Plus!

The Standard+Case Approach

Rob England

What people are saying about Plus! The Standard+Case Approach

Rob England's latest book *Plus! The Standard+Case Approach*, does in one short reading what many books attempt to accomplish in several years. S+C redefines the relationship for technology professionals by creating a route to customer experience, an improved skillset for ICT and redefines everything we thought we understood about "routine". Easy to read, effortless to consider, S+C brings a level of sanity back into the hyperbolic world of buzzword, out of touch, business related jargon. Slow down, this is one case you need to consider.

Chris Dancy, Founder, ServiceSphere

By tying together the mature practices of ITSM and Case Management Rob has strengthened and filled in gaps of both frameworks. A must read for ITSM professionals!

Troy DuMoulin, VP Consulting Services, Pink Elephant

Great reading and concept. Now I want to build it.

Matt Beran, ITSM consultant, co-host ITSM Weekly Podcast

Liberate yourself from the shackles of rigid process-based response management and improve customer satisfaction by applying Standard+Case

Mark Smalley, IT Paradigmologist, Capgemini and ASL BiSL Foundation

The simple structure of the prose and logic make it a pleasure to read and an excellent reference for those for whom Standardization - while is a vast improvement over chaos - is becoming a constraint.

Martin Erb, Pink Elephant

SEE SERVICE RESPONSE IN A NEW LIGHT

Plus! The Standard+Case Approach

© Copyright 2013 Two Hills Ltd

Created and published by Two Hills

     letterbox@twohills.co.nz

     www.twohills.co.nz

     PO Box 57-150, Mana

     Porirua 5247

     New Zealand

ISBN-13: 978-1482061741

Many thanks to all those who helped with this book, including Patsy Anderson, Ian Baxter, John Beachboard, Matt Beran, David Cannon, Troy DuMoulin, Brian Dunbar, Martin Erb, James Finister, Dave van Herpen, Matthew Hooper, Paul Jay, Ivor Macfarlane, Hank Marquis, Simone Moore, Rick Noble, Mark O'Loughlin, Barclay Rae, Stuart Rance, Tom Rankin, Mark Smalley, Antonio Valle, and Roger Williams. Thank-you and my apologies to all the others who I have missed off this list – so many have contributed ideas to this book.

Thanks to Charles Betz for pointing me to Case Management.

And a special thank-you to Thomas Davenport and Keith Swenson for their influential books on (see bibliography).

Table of Contents

A New Paradigm

Standard+Case is an exciting new paradigm for categorising and resolving any sort of response "tickets", such as service desk requests (including incidents), problems, or operational changes. The phrase "a new paradigm" gets much over-used but this time it applies. This approach changes the way we think about everything to do with response.

Standard+Case, or "S+C" for short, is a universal approach to responding to situations. Although Standard+Case applies to any response situation anywhere, this book is written primarily from the perspective of Information Technology Service Management (ITSM). Don't let that put you off if you work in another field: there is very little geek-speak here and the content can be generalised to any context.

The Standard+Case approach will improve your service response without a great deal of impact or investment in your current ITSM practices and systems.

Much of our thinking in IT Service Management is drawn from manufacturing, and focuses on standardisation (definition, repeatability) and statistical improvement of repeated tasks. But we no longer live in an industrial economy; we live in a service economy – hence Service Management. IT doesn't manage industrial production lines; it manages the delivery of services to people. People cannot to be standardised. Much of our traditional ITSM tries to make them be standardised: to engage users in a standard manner, to respond back to them in equally standard ways. ITSM pretends the world is standardised. When it is not - when non-standard things happen - ITSM treats them as exceptions, and as failures of the system. Think of long-running incidents, or requests that do not fall into any defined category. As a consequence, non-standard responses are poorly controlled, misleadingly reported, and no formal practices exist; so there is minimal structured improvement of how we deal with them.

Standard+Case acknowledges reality: much of our service activity will always be non-standard and has to be dealt with in a formalised way in order to manage, report and improve it as we do for the standardised part. We do that by treating non-standard responses as cases.

Standard+Case accepts that much of the service world is non-standard. It is not a new way of responding to situations; it is simply a new way of looking at what we do now. We do respond to non-standard situations now, but we have little rigour around who and how. Standard+Case formalises and brings rigour to our ad-hoc response, so that <u>all</u> instances of service response are managed, reported and improved, not just the standard ones.

As a result, Standard+Case is not introducing much that is new to traditional ITSM and it is certainly not replacing what we have now in ITSM practices. Standard+Case illuminates ITSM – it looks at it in a fresh way that better reflects reality. It validates the factory-floor approaches as valuable for the standard stuff, but also validates the non-standard responses as "normal". It does extend ITSM a little by introducing the concepts of Case Management to better deal with the non-standardised world which is so ad-hoc right now. And over time it standardises as much of the non-standard activity as possible. So the Standard+Case approach will improve your service response without a great deal of impact or investment in your current ITSM practices and systems.

Despite decades of growing sophistication in ITSM, customer and user satisfaction with IT support remain generally low. Standard+Case seeks to increase flexibility of response and better handle complex and unusual situations, in order to better serve customers. Our traditional ITSM approaches

> …struggle when it comes to addressing lower volume, unpredictable and sometimes highly complex requests. This is however the current customer service pain point and is where customer service champions excel … through the empowerment of their employees.[1]

Standard+Case is a step-change in our thinking about IT Service Management[2]. It is about applying a body of knowledge called Case Management to ITSM, synthesising it with our existing process-centric approach.

It addresses criticisms of ITSM approaches like ITIL[3] for being too process-centric and not allowing customers and knowledge workers to be empowered to get the job done. Many IT professionals see ITSM as the imposition of constraints - stifling creativity and innovation.

Standard+Case applies to anything that requires a human response: there's either a standard response or there isn't.

Standard+Case does not seek to replace or change ITIL or other theory: it expands and clarifies that theory to provide a more complete description of managing responses. The Case side of Standard+Case provides a space for people to demonstrate expertise, initiative and originality.

Standard+Case provides a good growth path for service desk analysts, which fits well with gamification - a hot topic right now in ITSM (see later in this book).

---

[1] *Using Case Management to Empower Employees and transform Customer Service*, Kofax, www.kofax.com

[2] The definitive description of service management, IT or otherwise, is the *USMBOK, Guide to the Universal Service Management Body of Knowledge*, I Clayton. See bibliography

[3] ITIL® is a Registered Trade Mark and a Registered Community Trade Mark of the UK Cabinet Office in the United Kingdom and other countries. The IT Infrastructure Library is a publication suite produced by the British Government over the last 20 years, now owned by the UK Cabinet Office http://www.best-management-practice.com/IT-Service-Management-ITIL/. There are no good online introductions to ITIL, in the author's opinion. Wikipedia is awful, bordering on wrong. See the bibliography.

Standard+Case is applicable to Problem Management and Change Management (and Event Management...) as well as Service Desk activities.

In fact, although this book has an IT perspective, Standard+Case applies to anything that requires a human response: there's either a standard response or there isn't.

Consider how we deal with responses in "classical" IT Service Management. By "responses" I mean Request, Incident, Problem, Change, Event ... any "ticket" which requires a human response. If you read the ITIL books or just about any other body of work on ITSM, it talks about following a process for dealing with the response, and the process comes from predefined models of how to deal with them. The design of this approach is based on Business Process Modelling (BPM).

If we encounter an unfamiliar "exception" condition, most guidance gets vague: it turns into a fuzzy cloud that says "resolve it". Problem Management is an area where almost every "ticket" is a previously unknown condition, so Problem Management guidance tends to have more information about dealing with un-defined situations, but the guidance is still generally vague outside of some formalism around root cause analysis.

I had been puzzling about how to deal with these non-standard exception conditions. A light went on reading this from the Workflow Management Coalition [1]:

> [Business Process Modelling] and [Case Management] are useful for different kinds of business situations.
>
> Highly predictable and highly repeatable business situations are best supported with BPM.
>
> For example signing up for cell phone service: it happens thousands of times a day, and the process is essentially fixed.
>
> Unpredictable and unrepeatable business situations are best handled with [Case Management].
>
> For example investigation of a crime will require following up on various clues, down various paths, which are not predictable beforehand. There are various tests and procedures to use, but they will be called only when needed.

Case Management is about managing "cases", where each new situation must be dealt with differently. Cases are dealt with by knowledge workers, known sometimes as case workers or case managers. Examples are medical, crime, legal, social work, audits, emergency responses, military attacks ... as well as many IT requests, incidents, problems and changes that don't fit a predefined business process model.

There is too much emphasis on efficiency and not enough on effectiveness.

---

[1] http://www.xpdl.org/nugen/p/adaptive-case-management/public.htm

Approaches derived from manufacturing methods - such as ITIL, Lean, TQM, or Six Sigma - don't work so well for knowledge workers. There is too much emphasis on efficiency and not enough on effectiveness. E.g. this resonated with me[1]:

> The system has to be ready when the flow comes: you need the idle resources that BPM or LEAN want to cut as waste

And this[2]:

> It cannot be assumed that ensuring a consistent result at lowest cost also improves process quality from a customer perspective, because it removes the ability to individualise and focus on customer perceived value and satisfaction

Knowledge workers find those process-centric regimented approaches de-humanising. They also find them out of step with their own experiences providing expert responses to complex situations.

Manufacturing methods only work for one group of the situations we face in service management: the well-understood, pre-defined, familiar ones.

The other group of response situations are unknown or unfamiliar: they present unique new situations every time. A BPM-based approach tries to deal with this group through Events[3], defining how to respond to external stimuli. Even if we were psychic enough to predict every "Event-uality", the resulting process model would be too complex to use.

Of course we can't predict. Each individual case is unique. Cases require expert knowledge workers who are empowered to address the situation dynamically as it unfolds.

To compound the issue, increasing usage of user self-service help and provisioning tools and mutual community support amongst end-users means that the responses required from our human staff are increasingly the complex non-standard situations. The users are resolving more of the standard ones themselves.

We must stop thinking all responses can be standardised. It is imperative that we acknowledge the existence of non-standard responses. In fact we need to go much further: we must enable our staff, design our practices, and select our tools in order to better manage and resolve these undefined unexpected cases. That is what Standard+Case does for us.

Before we can talk more about Standard+Case, we need to look at the two ideas behind it: Standard Models and Case Management.

---

[1] http://isismjpucher.wordpress.com/2011/12/11/adaptive-case-management-basic-full-or-strategic/

[2] *The Strategic Business benefits of Adaptive Case Management*, M.Pucher, *How Knowledge Workers get Things Done*, L. Fischer Ed., Future Strategies 2012, ISBN 978-0-9849764-4-7

[3] This BPM usage of "Event" is a broader use of the term than in the ITIL context.

Standard Models

Service Management practices are process-centric - certainly in ITSM they are. Business Process Modelling (BPM) concepts are central to the management of ITSM practices.

One of the core process concepts which is accepted and adopted within IT practices - almost without question - is the Capability Maturity Model. CMM (or the more modern CMMI) is based on the same premise as improvement methodologies like ITIL, Six Sigma, Lean, or in their own way DevOps and Agile. The premise is that to improve our performance we must make our processes more rigorously defined, driving them to be as repeatable as possible; then we must manage and measure the processes as tightly as possible. This is very much the industrial thinking that had its origins in "scientific management", or Taylorism: time-and-motion studies and so on. The benefits of such a formalised approach include:

- greater efficiency
- reduced costs
- faster response
- greater accountability
- better compliance
- better quality control, more accuracy
- better historical records
- fact-based (statistically driven) improvement
- more potential for automation

This rigour reached its peak in ITSM with ITIL. ITIL promotes the concept of CMM-style standardised processes in IT operations, especially for dealing with Request, Incident, Problem, and Change. For all these entities there is a generic response-handling process that goes like this:

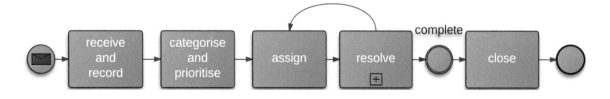

ITIL has the concept of "Models"– i.e. repeatable procedures - to deal with the ticket, depending on the category. Another in-vogue term within IT is "patterns". Mostly these models describe what to do in the Resolve step – the other steps will be much the same for all models: bag it, tag it, assign it to someone, and after it is dealt with close it.

ITIL talks about models for dealing with Requests[1] and Incidents[2] and Changes[3], and even Problems[4] - though model Problems will be rarer just because of the nature of Problems: we hopefully don't encounter the same ones too often. Since Event Management is a response process, one assumes you can have Event Models too, though ITIL doesn't explicitly mention them.

ITIL also talks about Incident models and some Change models being "Standard". In the case of Change, Standard also means pre-approved, but the aspect we care about is that "Standard" means that it is well understood, repeatable, and pre-defined. Standard means there is a document or online workflow or script or decision tree that tells you how to deal with that category of ticket, e.g. setting up a new user, or assessing an insurance claim, or ordering someone a new laptop.

S+C doesn't reject the standardising approach of BPM and CMMI and ITIL. On the contrary, we embrace it as *half* of our paradigm; we adopt the term "Standard Model" as a generic term for a standardised repeatable procedure for the resolution of a category of ticket.

For the purposes of our S+C approach, a Standard Model must be:

- **assessed on risk** not scale of activity. Big activities can be standardised if they are deemed to be acceptably low risk, and small-scale activities aren't automatically standard ones until proven to be low risk.

- **repeatable**. It is performed consistently within quality bounds e.g. Six Sigma.

- **fully documented and tested** in advance as a package: this is the "standard" bit.

- **unambiguously defined**. Before you "open the case door" and set staff free from Standard process constraints, it has to be agreed and clear what constitutes standard activity and what doesn't.

Note: Adaptive Case Management (see "Adaptive") talks about "templates" as guides to how to resolve a case. These can be thought of as partial models, or models that have yet to be standardised. We could call templates "non-standard models", or stick with the ACM terminology of "templates".

---

[1] ITIL 2011 *Service Operation* 4.3.4.2, 4.3.5.7

[2] ITIL 2011 *Service Operation* 4.2.4.2

[3] ITIL 2011 *Service Transition* 4.2.4.5

[4] ITIL 2011 *Service Operation* 4.4.4.2

Falling off the page

Standard response models do not deal with all situations. In the real world we face a situation, and as we run down our list of categories, procedures, workflows, checklists, templates or models, we find that this one is unfamiliar – it is not standardised.

Hank Marquis describes this[1] as "falling off the bottom of the page". Or to use a programming analogy, we fall through a series of logic tests and fail to match it with something.

Quite often in actual practice we try to act as if the world is standardised. We adopt industrial factory-floor approaches. We introduce static categorisation taxonomies. We measure people according to pre-determined models of what they should be doing.

The world does not work like that. Only tightly controlled, well-understood circumstances can be reduced to industrial production lines. IT development is not like that:

> Software development is most certainly not like manufacturing... No person with knowledge of manufacturing would argue that software can be produced on an assembly line... The running application is the assembly line, manufacturing transactions... For building (not running) systems, if we are seeking industrial analogies, then we need to look upstream of the manufacturing operation to product development[2]

Likewise IT service response cannot be entirely standardised. Humans are unpredictable and the IT world is too complex to completely understand or describe.

When this does not work out in reality, we grow frustrated with the exceptions that keep breaking our rules: responses that don't fit the categories; staff who respond in a non-standard manner because they felt they had to break the rules to get a result for the user; long-running responses that don't get resolved.

This failure of standardised approaches is because the world is non-standard. Human needs are complex. The world changes constantly, and fast. If we are to deal with it effectively, we need to extend our model beyond Standard. We need to accept that we are doing a lot of work now outside the Standard models. We must stop acting as if that isn't so and stop viewing the non-standard work as an exception. We need to recognise the other side to response. That's where Case Management comes in – for when we get to the bottom of the page.

---

[1] Private correspondence with the author

[2] *Architecture & Patterns for IT*, Charles T. Betz, Morgan Kaufmann 2011, ISBN 978-0-12-385017-1

This page intentionally left blank (except that it is not blank now).

Case Management

As we already mentioned, Case Management is a widely understood concept in a number of sectors, such as emergency services, medicine, social work, law, and policing.

It has been discussed within the IT world at times but it is not widely understood and adopted within IT in the same way that Service Management is now. (Arguably, some of those other sectors that use Case Management could benefit in return by learning more about Service Management and BPM from IT, which is the thought-leading sector right now in those disciplines.)

Knowledge workers have been around forever, but they now account for a third of workers or more in modern economies. Case Management is the main approach used by knowledge workers, and it depends on the abilities of those knowledge workers. There is a fundamental difference from the process-centric approach of ITSM today. Process improvement often starts from the premise of external experts improving the way work is done. Case Management starts from the premise that knowledge workers know what they are doing better than anyone else and need to be allowed to do it.

Case Management allows knowledge workers to manage the case professionally and dynamically as it unfolds. It is management's role to inform the case workers of the organisation's objectives and policies, so that they can make their own decisions; and to provide the case workers with sufficient resources to be successful. This aligns nicely with Drucker's principle[1] of "Management By Objectives".

Forrester[2] see three categories of Case Management emerging:

- service requests (human communications): e.g. loans, claims, underwriting, benefits, new customers.

- incident management (event-driven): e.g. healthcare, complaints, disputes, exceptions.

- investigative (transparency): e.g. due diligence, compliance, fraud detection, audit.

These are driven by customer experience, cost control, and risk mitigation.

---

[1] Drucker, *The Practice of Management*

[2] *Dynamic Case Management – an Old Idea Catches Fire*, C Le Clair and C Moore, Forrester 2009

Case Management has the following characteristics:

1. A case is a situation to be dealt with, e.g. a medical case, a legal case, a crime.

2. A case has a series of states and a goal(s); not a process, steps or a lifecycle.

3. The states are determined dynamically as the situation unfolds.

4. External events can change the state.

5. A case has a subject and the actions performed for that subject to achieve the result.

6. There are multiple options for what to do at each state. The selected actions are determined dynamically as the situation unfolds.

7. Some of those actions might be well-understood, pre-defined procedures (sub-processes).

8. Actions will involve the use of resources, which the case worker chooses dynamically. The case worker assembles resources as necessary. Resources include templates, checklists, content, policy, procedures, tools, people...

9. The states, actions, and resources are unpredictable.

10. Even the goals will change as the case develops.

11. So planning is part of execution, not a design activity (mostly). That planning may or may not be formalised as project management.

12. A case can still have decision gateways or milestones, but these need to be planned dynamically, or at least have some flexibility.

13. Because process is loose or undefined, good policy is essential, in order to define the principles, rules, bounds and guidelines.

14. A case has an owner (case worker) and a currently assigned individual or individuals performing the actions.

15. Data is central. Case Management is driven by data, with process secondary (the opposite of BPM).

16. Because Case Management is data driven, Change Management is integral to execution, in order to approve, control, and keep track of dynamic changes to that data.

17. Input and output data is added as necessary (although there may be outputs defined by goals or policy, and inputs required by policy or procedures).

18. Data will be large volumes of unstructured data in a wide variety of formats.

19. Collaboration between people is integral to quick effective resolution of a case.

20. Visibility and record of communications between all parties is an essential part of the data.

21. Enterprise architecture is required as an input to Case Management, to define business (markets, channels, partners...), organisation, capabilities, processes, IT.

22. Security is about auditability not just authentication: as well as approving access to data and systems, we also need to keep records of access.

23. A case usually ends - it is resolved (eventually) – but we must also deal with "cold cases".

Adaptive

There is an Adaptive Case Management movement that looks at adaptive IT systems to extend process management to be able to support Case Management[1] in any sector. Case Management is "Adaptive" when the ACM system changes in response to the external environment to make Case Management more successful, learning from past cases to improve stored knowledge, templates, checklists or procedures. This point seems to be misunderstood by some folk. Just because the plan, goals, actions, resources and so on dynamically change during an individual case doesn't make it "adaptive" in the ACM sense. Case Management is adaptive when the models and resources adapt based on the learnings of past cases in order to improve dealing with future cases. [2]

Here is the resulting feedback loop:

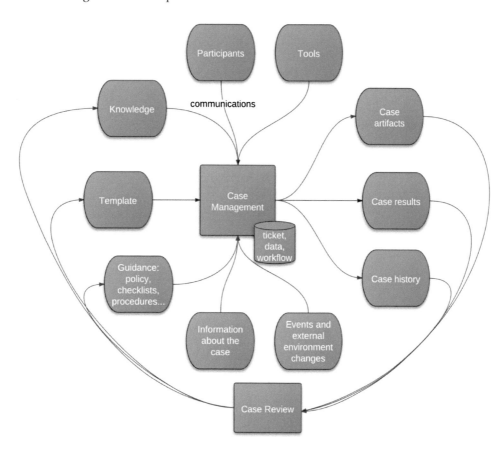

ACM comes more from the perspective of building on Business Process Modelling, and hence focuses on the development side of IT rather than operational practices. This book is more focused on ITIL and the service management disciplines. Also, ACM is quite tools-centric, whereas I

---

[1] From the Workflow Management Coalition http://www.xpdl.org/nugen/p/adaptive-case-management/public.htm

[2] see Max Pucher's *The Difference between DYNAMIC and ADAPTIVE*
http://acmisis.wordpress.com/2010/11/18/the-difference-between-dynamic-and-adaptive/

believe successful service provision must look at people, culture and practices. However there is clearly a lot in common, and this book draws from ACM.

As we will see, the combination of Standard and Case approaches takes this adaptability to a higher level. (See "Review and Improve")

Human Interaction Management

There is another approach that can be used when considering Case, called Human Interaction Management (HIM)[1], which de-emphasises process (as embodied in BPM) and emphasises five human factors. These are expressed in an abstract theoretical way in Harrison-Broninski's book[2], but mercifully he has rephrased them online[3] in more practical form:

- team building

- communication

- knowledge

- empowered time management

- collaborative, real-time planning

Of course the vendors have not missed the opportunity to provide a software element to HIM as well: there are tools that support these HIM interactions between people.

Korhonen[4] talks about HIM as defining roles, a story, and agreements. That is, there is a description of how responses are expected to play out, what performances are expected, and what agreements are negotiated as it unfolds.

---

[1] http://human-interaction-management.info/

[2] *Human Interactions: the Heart and Soul of Business Process Management*, Harrison-Broninski. See bibliography.

[3] http://harrison-broninski.com/keith/him/HIM-quick-reference-card.html

[4] *BPM – A Systemic perspective*, Janne J. Korhonen, EDS 2006 (presentation slides from the internet)

Chapter

4

The Standard+Case Approach

The combination of Standard and Case concepts gives a complete description of response handling, for any sort of activity that requires a human response.

- **Standard responses** are predefined because they deal with a known situation. They use a standardised process (and procedures) to deal with that situation. They can be modelled by BPM, controlled by workflow, and improved by the likes of Six Sigma, Lean IT and ITIL.

- **Case responses** present an unknown or unfamiliar situation where there is no predefined process. Cases demand knowledge, skills and professionalism of the person dealing with them. They are best dealt with by Case Management, being knowledge-driven and empowering the operator to decide on suitable approaches, tools, procedures and process fragments.

We look for a standard model of how to deal with a situation. If we can't find one, then we switch to dealing with it as a case. That's Standard+Case.

That gives us two complementary approaches to dealing with any situation that requires response: one or other approach will be suitable. A computer operator monitoring a console knows how to deal with a failed SAN disk so they take the standard action, but an unfamiliar message from a server causes them to pass it to an expert.

For the visual amongst us, when we combine the generic Standard process we talked about in "Standard Models" with Case Management, the process will now look like this:

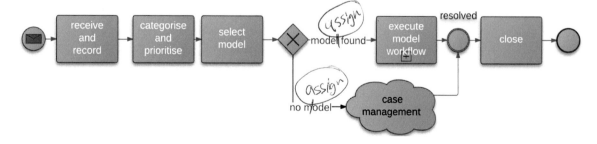

The process stays the same up until we look for a model to deal with the response, where we take either the Standard or Case branch for the Resolve step of the process. For more details, see "Process".

13

Let us contrast some of the characteristics of the Standard approach and the Case approach:

Standard	Case
Standard responses are:	**Case responses are:**
Routine	Unique
Predictable, repeatable	Non-repeated, unpredictable
Performed by trained process workers	Performed by knowledge workers
Outcomes are standardised and predefined	Outcomes are tailored to the user/client
View is focused	View is holistic
Tell workers WHAT and HOW	Tell workers WHAT and WHY
Serves the needs of the customer and the business	Serves the needs of the user and the support worker
The organisation as an organism	The enterprise as a community[1]
Defined, designed and planned in advance	Emergent: the plan and workflow unfold as the case goes along
Revolve around the procedural sequence of steps; and transfer of assignment between people/groups	Revolve around available knowledge and accumulated information about the case; and collaboration between people/groups
Controlled by the process designer and owner	Controlled by the participants
Documented at design time	Documented as the case progresses
Can (and should) be process-modelled	Cannot be process-modelled (note that Case Management will have a process wrapped around it)
Candidates for automation (if frequent and similar enough)	Cannot be automated (though pieces can)
Candidates for analysis and optimisation using statistics and observation	Can analyse and optimise by reviewing on a case-by-case basis
Fragile in the face of unfamiliar exception conditions	Robust in the face of unfamiliar exception conditions

---

[1] *Russell L. Ackoff, iconoclastic management authority, advocates a "systemic" approach to innovation,* , R. Allio, Strategy & Leadership Volume 31 issue 3, Emerald 2003

Yin and Yang

The two approaches of Standard and Case complement and complete each other: "Yin and Yang". Together they complete the circle. There is either a known standard response or there isn't.

Of course the world isn't so black-and-white. Standard and Case are in fact the opposite ends of a spectrum of possible approaches. Some cases might have a certain level of process structure; some standard process models might allow flexibility. Nevertheless the Standard+Case model is more crisply delineated than some other two-sided models that still serve us perfectly well in practice, e.g. customer vs. supplier, innocent vs. guilty, working vs. on holiday.

Many dichotomies (pairings) have been compared to Standard+Case, such as

- incident + problem

- Level 1 + Level 2 support

- engineered + agile

- simple + complex (see "Scope/Context")

- deductive + inductive reasoning

- off-the-hook + bespoke tailoring, i.e. make to stock + make to order[1]

- robust + anti-fragile[2]

… which all have some correspondence to Standard thinking and Case thinking, respectively. Beware though: none of them correspond exactly. Some help us understand Standard+Case better but others could be a misleading comparison. Philosophers are invited to think about this further, and engage the author in discussion if you wish.

There is no "completeness theorem" for Standard+Case. That is, we do not <u>prove</u> the assertion that the Standard approach plus the Case approach cover <u>all</u> possible situations. What is asserted without proof is that in the real world a very high proportion of situations can be handled effectively by one approach or the other, or a combination or hybrid of the two.

Most people who have worked in response situations will agree with this. You look for the standard, predefine way of dealing with the situation; if you can't find one you manage the situation until you can find an answer. What we are doing in the latter situation is Case Management, whether we call it that or not. Standard+Case simply recognises that fact and formalises it, so that our planning, resourcing, management, monitoring and improvement look at the whole picture and deal with all situations we face not just the standard ones.

---

[1] The model is more complex than just these two approaches to manufacturing, as Charles Betz describes in an IT context http://www.lean4it.com/2010/05/large-it-considered-as-engineer-to-order-manufacturing.html and http://www.lean4it.com/2010/10/two-dimensions-of-production.html#more

[2] *Antifragile: Things That Gain from Disorder*, N Taleb, Random House 2012, 978-1400067824. Don't try to read it: research anti-fragile online.

Synergy

When we combine conventional service management response process, Standard response models, and the principles of Case Management for resolving non-standard situations, the sum is greater than the parts. Not only do we get a more complete description of how response procedures really work, we get new opportunities that none of the approaches on their own present.

For example, we talked about Adaptive Case Management, where the review process captures improvements to knowledge, templates, and guidance. Standard+Case takes that to a new level. As part of improving templates for Case, we identify new Standard models and capture them for future response situations which will be dealt with using a Standard not Case approach. In other words, not only does S+C adapt by improving the Case resources (the ACM approach), it also adapts by adding new Standard models: we constantly drive future workload from Case to Standard (see "Adapt").

This is profoundly important, because it allows our response capability to adapt to changing external circumstances such as new or changed services, new technologies in the consumer market, new customer markets, new groups of users, and so on.

Benefits

Trying to impose Standard systems of execution, measurement, reporting and accountability to non-standard situations is counterproductive. Allowing people to do case work when appropriate will increase efficiency and effectiveness by getting process out of the way when it is not applicable. Experienced experts don't like to be told what to do.

We also increase performance by formalising and optimising the situation that already exists. When Standard models run out, what staff do now is ad-hoc Case Management without recognising it as that, and without any formal guidance, rules, resources or methods. Applying some formality to Case Management means we can begin to get useful metrics, to do useful reviews, and to put in place improvement mechanisms to get better at it over time.

Case Management improves morale as staff get empowerment, seniority, recognition and freedom. They work to a new definition of success that recognises the realities of dealing with non-standard cases, removing some of the frustrations of being measured using the wrong metrics.

Most of all, having a Case alternative to formal process allows staff to handle non-Standard requests (and changes) from users. That means the customer is empowered as well as the worker: the users are allowed to ask for things that are not in the request catalogue. The customer will agree with the provider what the policy is, what the bounds and rules are. The case worker will operate within those limits to meet the non-standard needs of the users. The result is a much higher standard of service: more "willing", more flexible, with better fulfilment of user needs.

Risk

Clearly there are risks in not having a defined procedure to deal with situations, or - more precisely - not having defined procedure for certain steps in dealing with situations (recall that most or all of case management happens in the Resolve step of the defined process). However, Case Management can be seen as simply formalising what happens now, when staff "fall off the bottom" of Standard procedures, yet have no alternative formalised approach. Therefore we are not increasing risk by introducing Case; we are (hopefully) reducing risk by introducing some formalised structure and controls to an otherwise uncontrolled situation.

Nevertheless certain risks remain.

Unresolved cases

Standard+Case makes it more acceptable that a ticket should stay open for an extended period. It recognises that cases take longer and may be insoluble: this is not perceived as a failure of the system because cases are unpredictable. Will this mean that staff will try less hard to resolve cases than they would if long-running tickets are reported as a failure of service levels? There is no data yet, so this remains a matter of opinion. Given that the most professional staff are assigned to cases, one would hope not.

One mitigation is to reward and praise those who close long-running cases (as compared to negatively assessing the owners of open ones, which is counter-productive).

Another mitigation to this and some of the following risks is that formalising the Case Management practice brings greater awareness of scrutiny and more peer interaction, which activates case workers' sense of social and organisational responsibilities.

Over-spending

If case workers have the freedom to determine actions and goals, and to request and deploy resources, there is the risk of group budgets being exceeded and/or resources being depleted.

Policy for Standard+Case should include some form of budget or resource limits per case, a mechanism for requesting and allocating funds, and the monitoring of S+C should include resource consumption and costs.

Part of the Close step for all cases should be to report on costs and usage of resources.

Over-generous

There is a similar risk if case workers are free to determine the outcomes for their clients/users: that staff will become overly generous; that they will empathise with users and give away too much.

Mitigating this comes down to making more information available about the business priorities and requirements, and more transparency about business decision-making. If staff understand why certain rules or restrictions exist, they are more likely to consider them fair (see "Transparency"). They will take a balanced view of the needs of the user and the business.

The Review process should assess the appropriateness of the solutions delivered, and the overall costs, to ensure that case workers are controlling outlays within policy bounds.

Inappropriate use of the Case approach

If Standard+Case reduces the censure for long-running or unresolved cases, and makes available a wider range of actions and resources, then there will always be a high risk that staff will categorise a response as a Case when they should have used some Standard model procedure to resolve it.

Policy must make clear under what conditions it is permissible to use Case Management.

The Review step should consider whether Case was an appropriate approach to use. Inappropriate use of the Case approach should result in education, warning and eventually censure, including "demotion" to lose the certification to be a Case Worker.

Standard risks

Conversely, Case Management mitigates some of the risks of the Standard approach. The main risk of Standard is that we will not deliver what the user wants; instead we will deliver what the procedure specifies. That is, the lack of flexibility of Standard models does not allow us to respond to all types of user request.

By allowing staff the option to decide that no Standard model applies in a certain situation, we mitigate that risk by giving them the flexibility to be responsive.

Scope/Context

The Cynefin model[1] gives us a generic description of the world and how we deal with it[2]. It applies to systems (in the broadest sense), situations, and our responses.

The Cynefin framework has five domains:

- **Simple**: we know what to do for the recognised conditions, the situation is familiar, so we Sense & Categorise & Respond. Here we use best practice.

- **Complicated**: we know what the situation is but it is an unfamiliar one. It requires an expert to work out what to do. We Sense & Analyse & Respond. Here we allow the expert to select from a range of good practices.

- **Complex**: the situation is unknown. We need to explore and experimentally determine the practices that work. The approach is to Probe & Sense & Respond. We develop emergent practice.

- **Chaotic**: we can't know what is going on. We must move quickly to get some control. We Act & Sense & Respond. If we are lucky, we discover novel practice.

- **Disorder**: we don't know what the domain is. Typically people behave as if it were their preferred comfort domain.

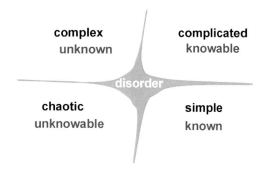

---

[1] http://en.wikipedia.org/wiki/Cynefin

[2] There are many other similar models. As well as the ones in this book, see also:

- Tom Graves' SCAN framework http://weblog.tetradian.com/tag/scan/

  Everyday Enterprise-Architecture: sensemaking, strategy, structures and solutions, T. Graves, Tetradian 2010, 978-1906681241

- Ralph Stacey's Agreement and Certainty Matrix http://business-survival-toolkit.co.uk/stage-three/change-management/the-agreement-certainty-matrix

- Jurgen Appelo's Simplicity model http://www.noop.nl/2010/09/simplicity-a-new-model.html

- Dee Hock's Chaordic model http://www.chaordic.org/definitions.html

One would use the Standard approach to deal with Simple situations and some Complicated ones, and Case Management to deal with the remaining Complicated and Complex situations and perhaps Chaotic conditions.

A booking for a training course is Simple. A request for a whole new course to be designed is Complicated. A request to invent a new way of delivering courses is Complex. A writ to shut the company down for copyright violations is Chaotic. Disorder is when their lawyers lock the doors and seize all the computers.

In the Complex situation we find ourselves in an unknown state so we have no techniques or knowledge to use as resources. We need to explore and learn how to deal with it.

In the Complicated situation, the state is knowable. I also call this "unfamiliar". We need to use existing resources to determine enough information to make the situation known, and possibly transform it into a Simple situation.

We can infer that there are in fact two types of case workers: experts to deal with a Complicated situation, and explorers to deal with Complex ones.

Another similar model is Davenport's classification of knowledge processes[1], which I reshape here to show the comparison with the Cynefin model:

Standard+Case challenges our desire to make life simple and defined. It just isn't. You can't standardise everything, no matter how you try. Does that make it harder to forecast, plan, manage, and budget? Sure. Welcome to real life.

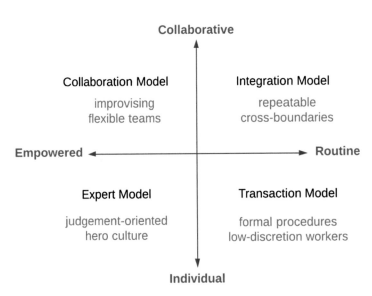

Standard+Case is about formalising the limits of what we can standardise, and ring-fencing the remaining non-standard stuff to minimise its impact and improve our handling of it.

---

[1] *Thinking for a Living.* See Bibliography

Policy

Before staff are "let off the leash" to be case workers planning and executing their own Case response, we must put in place new controls to mitigate the new risks introduced.

The most important control is policy. Policy defines the principles to operate by, some general goals, and the hard and soft rules, the bounds and guidelines. Those bounds will include specifying any compliance that is required, whether internal (architecture) or external (regulation).

Here is a great analogy from *Mastering the Unpredictable*: hard bounds are the guard-rails on the road, soft bounds are the painted white lines. It is OK to go outside the white lines although the advice is not to and everybody knows there is a risk associated with it, so they proceed with caution.

If you are going to set staff free without defined process or deliverables, policy is essential. It is essential for both the organisation and the individual case workers.

Policy mitigates risk for the organisation. It defines the limits beyond which certain actions will present an unacceptable risk. So we set the hard and soft bounds for Case Management: what people can and can't do; what they must document and what they shouldn't; where their authority extends; their budget.

Policy also ensures fairness for the staff. If you do not define what staff should not do, don't be upset if they do it. Policy gives them safety: they know what they are empowered to do.

Monitoring

In addition to introducing policy, the other essential risk control is to monitor the execution of case management. We want to monitor efficiency (performance), effectiveness (quality), and compliance with policy. To achieve this, we must modify our KPIs and assessment tools to acknowledge that Case Management is measured differently.

There are several ways to monitor Case Management:

- Statistical measurement. Metrics are considered in the "Measurement" section of this book, and their use in assessing how well we deliver are discussed in "Service Levels". See "Measurement" for more on metrics.

- Observation. Apply "corporate anthropology" to the study of case workers on the job ("in the wild"). Spend time with them understanding what they do and how they do it.

- Review. This book mentions the importance of the review step several times. We need a permanent review function (team, capability) that reviews selected cases and analyses, reports and acts on the results.

- Audit. In addition to the Review function, there is a need for forensic audit to ensure compliance to policy and law.

Beyond S+C

A spectrum

Standard+Case is a simplistic two-sided model. Organisations that use S+C may evolve over time to a more graduated approach, where Standard and Case are seen as the two ends of a spectrum of possible approaches to a response.

As the approach to responding becomes more sophisticated over time, the rules can allow limited degrees of freedom somewhere between Standard and Case. Workers following Standard models can have a degree of discretion and flexibility around how to respond depending on the situation and the needs of the user. Some standardisation of case work can be introduced to manage the amount of variation and improve quality.

Unknown and unfamiliar

Case Management is being used in this book as an umbrella description for dealing with responses to what Cynefin would classify as Complicated, Complex and Chaotic situations – all the situations except Simple ones.

Most of the time when we are managing a response it will be Simple, Complicated or Complex. Chaotic is a special case we will deal with later.

In some situations we do not have enough information to know if we can deal with the situation in a Standard way - it is Complex and Unknown. We must use our knowledge and skills to find out more, to better define the situation, to develop new discoveries and methods so that we can make it knowable. After we have enough information, we can determine whether it is a Complicated Knowable situation, or a Known Simple one. That would be a new state for the case: we have moved forward.

Note that the Standard+Case model is that we don't switch to Case Management until the Resolve step of the response-handling process. This means the diagnostic step is not using Case Management, even though we may be in an unknown state during the diagnosis: we are in the Disordered domain – we don't know what the state is. It is only if we progress through diagnosis and decide we cannot categorise the response, that the Resolve step then starts out in Unknown Complex state and moves into Case Management as the approach to resolving the situation.

In other situations we have enough information to know what we are dealing with, and to realise that we haven't dealt with this exact situation before. It is Complicated and Knowable - or as we say in this book, Unfamiliar. We need to apply our existing skills and techniques to work out how to resolve this particular situation. After we have enough information, we can fully define how to deal with it, to make it Known and Simple to deal with next time.

So with increasing sophistication in the application of Case Management, the Case approach can be split into two related approaches depending on whether the situation is Unknown or Unfamiliar, with different templates, techniques, and even different case workers.

Chaos

Chaotic situations are about all hell breaking loose: in other words the early stages of a Major Incident or a Discontinuity (i.e. a situation that Business Continuity plan for). These will be managed outside the realms of normal managed response: they will be managed by specialists and likely draw in resources from all teams in the organisation.

Major Incidents and Discontinuities go through a lifecycle from initial Disorder (we don't know what the state is) to increasingly more controlled situations (hopefully), or they spiral into Chaos (we do not control the state). They won't be Simple; every Major Incident will be a case. All the Case expertise, resources and techniques can be applied to them.

This would be a useful growth of Case Management capability over time: to contribute to Major Incident Management and Business Continuity Management.

Chapter 5

Service Management Case

Here is a summary of the important components of Case Management in a service management context (we will call it SM-Case), as distinct from other contexts such as medicine, social work, or policing, which have different needs and emphases. These are the aspects of Case which may be different from traditional ITSM or increased in importance:

- Strategy: case workers need to understand what the goals are and why they need to achieve them. They need transparency of the decision-making from the highest levels of the organisation down, so that they can make informed decisions within their cases.

- Policy: principles, goals, rules, compliance, bounds. If you empower people you *must* give them rules and bounds; otherwise it is unfair for them and dangerous for the organisation. (See Policy)

- Certify expert staff, and empower them to act as they see fit when managing a case (people have to earn and keep the status of "expert"). This changes how we do management, RACI, HR, security and so on... Certification is often essential: doctors handle cases, nurses handle Standard transactions.

- Manage varying levels of skill, e.g. through certification and gamification.

- Value and study diversity of approach. Standardised process discourages deviance, whereas S+C embraces it and studies the best and worst performers. Not only do we learn from the outliers; diversity in approaches gives us resilience to change. It acts like natural selection: as the environment changes, different approaches will be more successful.

- Support constant planning as well as doing.

- Planning happens before and during a case. Some prior generic planning can be done for certain situations, but because each case is unique, so too is the plan for how to deal with it. The military saying comes to mind: "No plan survives the first encounter". A plan may not survive to the end of the case – it may need to be torn up and done anew; and every plan will certainly evolve as new data comes to light or we reach an unexpected state.

- Provide access to as much diagnostic and resolution information as possible.

- Collaboration becomes much more important in Case: people need to work together to find answers quickly when there are no Standard answers.

- Standard and Case ticket tracking is preferably integral, performed in one tool or linked tools. Case is a branch to the process, not an independent activity (see "Process").

- Support emergent process: allow flexibility, the ability to create and change dynamic procedure (workflow) on the fly: add, link, branch, remove, or skip tasks; change assignments of tasks. The staff need to be empowered and skilled to reconfigure procedure; the policy should permit it and define the bounds; and the tools should support this functionality.

- Provide content management, and change management of that content.

- Provide and record communication between all parties. Note: this means email, messaging, and social interaction tools are only useful if we capture a permanent record.

- Archives and records management are required.

- Deadlines, reminders and calendaring are equally as important in Case as in Standard processing. Collaboration can mean complex parallel execution of tasks. We track progress by measuring time in each particular state.

- Monitor and manage a Case approach to the Resolve step using time, cost, and outputs - not completion of actions or their sequence.

- Have a strong review procedure for individual cases to identify improvements to knowledge and other resources (as compared to a focus on improvements to processes in a BPM model)

- Review and improve knowledge.

- Provide and constantly develop resources (see Resources):

  - templates: repeatable tasks; documents we expect to see; data we want

  - procedures, work instructions, or "mini-processes" that can be assembled by workers as required to perform repeatable tasks

  - checklists

  - knowledgebase

  - automation of the repeatable bits where appropriate (see Automation) e.g. calculations

- Tools and resources should embed policy rules, guidelines and bounds (business, legal, marketing, CRM...). They need access controls and audit trails to mitigate the freedom we give the case workers. This can often be fulfilled by simply documenting or linking to the rules – it does not necessarily imply automated enforcement (see Automation).

- The system should enforce as many of the rules as can be sensibly automated, but the system should only warn on soft rules.

Case+Standard

Why is Case the exception condition in Standard+Case's otherwise Standard approach to responding? Why not manage everything as a Case, with Standard templates available when required? I.e. why isn't it Case+Standard rather than Standard+Case?

Service Management has developed advanced disciplines of structure, control, measurement and improvement, which enable reductions in costs and increases in quality: improved efficiency and effectiveness.

It is not necessary or appropriate to abandon these advances. The conventional Service Management approach can still tightly manage all steps of the response processes except the Resolve step, and all instances of the Resolve step except where a Case approach is used.

This is not always desirable: some organisations with a strategy of exceptionally high response service levels will want to do "Case+Standard"; to have case workers handle everything up front and gate the tickets into Standard models where they can. It looks like this:

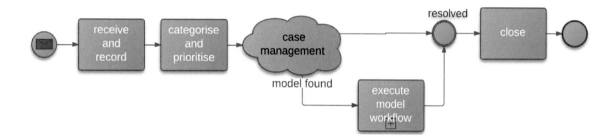

Service Levels

Service levels should ideally be measured according to customer-centric, outside-in metrics. One hopes that such measures will in fact improve with Case Management – that is the point: to get better at serving the customer by being more rigorous about how we handle the responses that drop off Standard processing.

We can use service level metrics like mean time to resolve for Standard response and mean time to change state for Cases - see "Measurement". But these metrics are internal "machinery" measurements. They are good for helping improve internally but they don't measure the service: they don't measure how happy customers are with the result, what the costs were, or how much value it delivered.

Outside-in, black-box measurements of service delivery like satisfaction, cost, and value will work well as service level targets in a Service Level Agreement (SLA), independent of whether we are applying a Standard or Case approach internally.

The very fact that "hard" tickets are being dealt with by expert case workers, and are producing some visible action and outputs, should improve external measures regardless of the "solve" rate.

We combine feedback from the users and from how we are tracking against the SLA targets as performance information. We combine that performance information with the internal operational metrics to determine what needs improving.

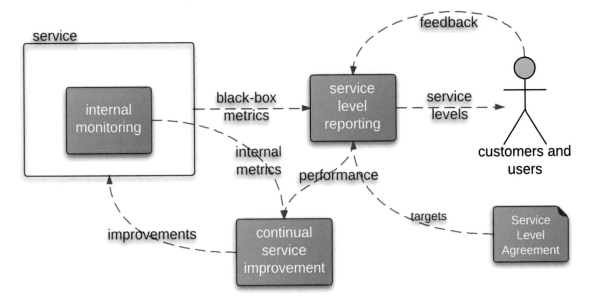

SLAs and time

The term "Service Level Agreement" is often misused. A Service Level Agreement (SLA) is an agreement (formal or informal, explicit or implicit) between two people or human groups. Every service has an SLA even if it is only implied or casually agreed. A Service Level Target (SLT) is a deliverable or metric within that SLA. The conventional service level targets for responsiveness are based on time to resolve, by priority.

Mean time to resolve a number of responses (e.g. per month) is a useful measure for trending and improvement but it is hardly a fair measure of how well a case worker team is performing. Measuring the number of responses that exceed a time threshold (the "long tail" of the distribution curve) is even less fair. And holding people accountable for the time to resolve any one response is less fair still. The service provider cannot be held to a target resolution time when the sequence of states for each case is unpredictable.

SLTs are not just metrics. They are metrics which people are held accountable for. If they are not fair then they won't have the desired effect, and time-based SLTs are unfair for Cases. The time to resolve is anyone's guess: each Case is unique and some are unsolvable. The time for a particular Case is out of any person's control.

Don't listen to some of the buzz in the ITSM industry: informal SLAs are a bad idea. Clear, agreed, documented expectations between parties are always a good idea in business. The negotiation of Service Level Agreements and their subsequent documentation must make clear that resolution-time targets only apply to Standard situations, and that other targets for responsiveness performance besides time will be used for Cases.

Customers might initially baulk at this. Explain that this is only reflecting reality, and that including the non-Standard situations in resolution times distorts the picture. By measuring only Standard responses, the targets can be more tightly predicted and measured.

Explain what we call the Fireman's Conundrum:

> If high priority incidents are to be resolved quickly while lower priority incidents can take progressively longer, this is akin to firemen promising to extinguish three-alarm fires within ten minutes but a backyard grassfire may take until tomorrow. It is absurd on three levels: extinguishing the fire takes as long as it takes, bigger fires take longer, and that little yard fire won't be so small tomorrow.

Also explain the Doctor's Conundrum:

> Doctors can't predict how long it will take on average to diagnose patients, let alone cure patients. Diagnosis may take any number of tests and consultations, and multiple opinions. Only a minority of illnesses are even identifiable. Then the cure depends on the diagnosis and even then it is inly predictable if the diagnosis turns out to be a known illness with a known treatment (Standard). Once again, the only thing the doctor can promise ahead of time is the *level of resourcing that will be applied* and the urgency of the response, depending on the severity of the symptoms.

In summary, we can commit to mean time to restore Standard responses (commit to shorter times and with more accuracy and confidence), and we can only commit to levels of resources (especially people) applied to Cases. These metrics can be set and measured for differing levels of priority as we do now. As we discussed above, there are better measures of service levels than time anyway, in any context. Times is a useful dial on internal dashboards, but let us move away from it when agreeing service levels with customers.

Longitudinal Case Management

Some sectors have the concept of longitudinal case management, especially the health and social welfare sectors. A case is a patient, who goes through a series of states and what we would call responses over time. Longitudinal management keeps a single picture of that patient over their lifecycle, managed as one case. What we have been calling a case is treated by longitudinal management as a "sub-case"; a period of time and a set of states within the longer history of the overall case.

Standard+Case is a generalised model for responding to all situations in service delivery. The idea of longitudinal management is most applicable to S+C where the subject is a person, though it could also be applicable to a physical asset, a piece of equipment. The value of longitudinal case management is in ensuring an optimal lifecycle for that person or asset to make the experience as consistent as possible, and to ensure that every situation has the context of the past history available to it.

The way most Service Management practice is structured, this would be a departure from how we approach dealing with people. Service Management tends to deal with people on three levels:

- **Executive**: contractual and service level agreements

- **Account**: regular contact and reporting with the customers (those paying for the service)

- **Support**: regular contact and support for users (those consuming the service)

In most Service Management, the longitudinal aspect of service delivery is Customer Relationship Management (CRM) which tends to be focused on that middle layer: account management of customers. The entity managed longitudinally by CRM is the customer and all their users as a group.

At the lowest of these three levels of engagement, it is different. Support functions sometimes have access to the user's previous history as information, but each situation is dealt with in isolation. It would be better, more outside-in, to deal primarily with the user and secondly deal with their incidents as part of the user experience i.e. to handle each user longitudinally over their "lifetime".

The other entity which ITSM often deals with over a lifecycle is the asset. The management of their lifecycle is again dealt with outside of response, i.e. outside of Service Support. When responding to a situation, the asset's lifecycle information is available but the situation is handled in isolation.

There is merit in a more longitudinal approach to IT's users and assets. It would improve user experience and it could make us better at case resolution. The trade-off will be greater cost and complexity, especially the impact on tool requirements for tracking and managing a longitudinal case.

Let us quote some sources from the health sector on longitudinal management, to demonstrate how it could apply to service management in general. I have taken these quotes and removed the sector-specific language from them:

> All [users] can benefit from the support and guidance of a service coordinator, a professional who can offer advice in a continuing manner and be available to monitor function over the years. .. With time, new questions inevitably emerge, as a [user's issues] evolve while … expectations undergo progressive change. Because [users] represent such a heterogeneous group, no two call for identical management plans. Nor is it possible to predict with certainty … what the needs of a [users] will be [in future]. Consequently, [users] require vigilant follow-up plus individualized, objective advice and informed advocacy throughout their years in [the organisation].[1]

> Case management is a procedure to plan, seek, and monitor services for different social agencies and staff on behalf of a client. Usually one agency takes primary responsibility for the client and assigns a case manager, who coordinates services, advocates for the client, and sometimes controls resources and purchases services for the client. The procedure allows many [case] workers in the agency, or in different agencies to coordinate their

---

[1] Expert Consult
http://www.expertconsultbook.com/expertconsult/ob/book.do?method=display&type=bookPage&decorator=none&eid=4-u1.0-B978-1-4160-3370-7..00055-9--s0290&isbn=978-1-4160-3370-7

efforts to serve a given client through professional teamwork, thus expanding the range of needed services offered.[1]

Case management focuses on delivering personalized services to [users] to improve their care, and involves four steps:

1) Referral of new [users] (perhaps from another service if the client has relocated to a new area out of previous jurisdiction, or if client no longer meets the target of previous service, such as requiring a greater level of care.

2) Planning & delivery of care

3) Evaluation of results for each [user] & adjustment of the care plan

4) Evaluation of overall program effectiveness & adjustment of the program [2]

Longitudinal management of the lifecycle of a customer's relationship with us means there will be multiple touch-points over time, across multiple users from that customer, using multiple channels. The interactions at those touch-points will be a mix of Standard and Case interactions. This is an area for potential improvement in IT Service Management.

ITIL

On the Standard to Case spectrum, ITIL leans more towards a process-centric Standard approach, using BPM and CMM. It attracts industrial process-optimisation techniques such as Lean and Six Sigma. But ITIL has some Case Management content too - especially in Problem Management - even if does not give it that label.

This "Case-like" content has always sat uncomfortably with ITIL's emphasis on process, measurement, continual service improvement, and CMM-style process-management maturity.

Standard+Case will help to resolve this conflict, by providing a formal construct for the "non-process" parts of ITIL. We can introduce rigour, structure, ownership, accountability, policy, controls, and measurement - for an area that currently slips outside of Service Management control to the frustration of all involved.

Incident Management

In an ITSM world, one of the most important *responses* is Incident Management. Incident Management is about restoring service to our users. It is a classic example of a response situation where Standard+Case can be applied. Many Incident situations are standardised: we know them

---

[1] Wikipedia http://en.wikipedia.org/wiki/Case_management_(USA_health_system)

[2] William F. Bluhm, "Group Insurance: Fourth Edition," Actex Publications, Inc., 2003 ISBN 1-56698-448-3, quoted on Wikipedia

already and we have pre-defined models for dealing with them. But a large number of incidents (probably the majority) are not familiar. We need to handle them as a case.

Incident Management – like any practice – is made up of plans, policies, skills, roles, teams, resources, tools, metrics and reporting as well as process and procedures. All of these should be focused on the user and their needs, and not on the underlying technical issues. I have written elsewhere[1] about how ITIL muddies Incident Management with other inward-facing activities focused on resolving technical causes of the incidents. These inward activities are Problem Management. If service is restored to the user by any means or the user loses interest, the incident should be considered resolved. This is the author's opinion.

If we follow this crisp definition of incidents as being wholly focused on the user, then standardisation is easier.

Problem Management

Problem Management is about removing the causes of incidents. ITIL tends to focus on removing the cause of future incidents but I think – as in the argument under Incident management above – that Problem Management is equally about removing the cause of current and past incidents. Problem Management is about resolving _all_ causes of Incidents – it is not Incident Management's job to do that. This is the author's opinion.

Few problems will be Standard: one would hope that familiar problems do not recur too often in most IT organisations. Most of the time a problem is a case. Traditional ITMS techniques for problem resolution are Case Management techniques, even if we haven't recognised them as such: root cause analysis, war rooms, ad-hoc teams…

Request Management[2]

In the ITIL world-view, if it is not an Incident and the user is asking for it then it is a Request. See the Appendices under Taxonomy for a more sophisticated way of categorising responses.

Requests are a mix of Standard and Case responses: the proportion varies by organisation. There is an implicit assumption in much ITSM thinking that all requests should be Standardised, e.g. that a request catalogue will cover all possible requests, or at least that any non-Standard request is an exception. We will discuss this assumption later in the book, but suffice to say that it is an ideal that is never attained. Users will ask for things that we haven't thought of or dealt with before. How we deal with that fact tells a lot about our real attitude to serving the user.

---

[1] _How ITIL gets Incident vs Problem wrong_ http://www.itskeptic.org/content/how-itil-gets-incident-vs-problem-wrong

[2] ITIL calls this "Request Fulfilment" which strictly speaking is only one process within Request Management. I stick to the more generic term "Request Management" in this book.

Change Management

"Change" is one of those words that IT uses and abuses with a wide range of meanings. In terms of responses, there are two main types of change:

- Request For Change (RFC): a customer proposes a new service or a variation to a service

- Operational Change: a change to a service is to be rolled into production or into another controlled environment, e.g. test or training

These are both responses, and they are quite different. They should be dealt with by different practices: different policy, goals, roles, teams, processes, procedures, tools, and metrics. But both types of change can be handled as Standard+Case.

Standard RFCs are not that common – most RFCs are a case: they need to be evaluated and a custom solution needs to be worked out. If it is a standard change to a service that is being requested, it is usually handled by Request Management instead.

Standard operational changes have a special meaning in ITIL: a Standard Change is one that is not only standardised but also therefore pre-approved. Is every non-pre-approved operational change a Case? You can argue yes or no – this is an organisational decision.

> On one hand, we may have a model for how to do certain operational changes but they still need approval. The change is highly standardised in the Standard+Case sense but it is not an ITIL Standard Change.

> On the other hand, this could get confusing so you may choose to treat all non-pre-approved changes as Cases: each one needs to be evaluated on its merits in order to determine what needs to be done and in order to approve it. In this scenario, Standard Change means the same thing in ITIL and S+C.

DevOps

The concepts of DevOps and its relatives Lean IT, TQM and Six Sigma originate from industrial manufacturing. They depend on improving and automating repeatable standardised activities, i.e. they apply to standard responses – mostly changes and releases. Some may see DevOps as being about the complex or chaotic situations but I beg to differ.

DevOps is built around the concept of "anti-fragile"- from the book of the same name[1] by Nicholas Taleb. That is not to say that DevOps grew out of anti-fragile. DevOps arose before the book came out – Taleb just gave that principle a name. DevOps called it agility.

---

[1] *Antifragile: Things That Gain from Disorder*, N Taleb, Random House 2012, ISBN-13: 978-1400067824

DevOps is a natural outgrowth of Agile development: as development produces faster iterations of code, they need to be released into production just as quickly. Anti-fragile is the concept that true resiliency comes not from making a system robust in order to resist change, but by making it flexible to adapt to change, as quickly as possible –anti-fragile systems thrive on disorder.

In code terms, this means that instead of trying to prevent every possible production error, DevOps aims to fix any errors that slip through within a very short period of time. Instead of the concept of emergency changes, the fixes roll through in the next high-frequency automated release. DevOps emphasises the value in reducing the size of changes to minimise the size of errors and hence to reduce the risk of a catastrophic result. In fact such deployment systems may include the concept of a "chaos monkey": an automated piece of code that deliberately breaks services at random, in order to test them and strengthen them.

Another foundational principle of DevOps is "infrastructure as code", meaning the automated provisioning of the required infrastructure for the applications (usually taking advantage of Cloud IaaS or virtualisation by means of scripts) so that the infrastructure and the application can be released as one build of code together.

In order to push changes at this speed and frequency, the release of those changes must be automated: the build, multi-stage testing, and production turnover. In order to achieve this level of automation, such changes must be highly standardised. DevOps is all about Standard Change. A change to a system that did not have this automation in place - that had to be manually built, tested and deployed - would be handled outside DevOps as a Case.

Development

Development is not really a "response". It could be argued that a development project is a response to user requirement, but I prefer to see the initiating of the project to do the development as the response. Treating development projects as responses stretches the concept too much: Standard+Case is not really applicable to development, whether it is agile or waterfall in approach.

Standard+Case is applicable to the responses that happen within the development lifecycle: the initial requests, the RFCs, and the operational changes.

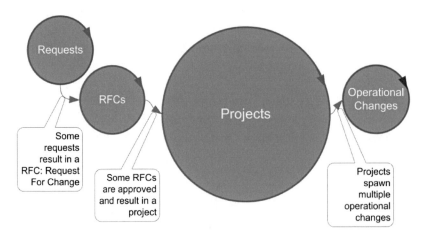

Chapter 6

People

One of the favourite mantras in ITSM is "People Process Technology[1]". ITSM says that these are three important aspects that must be considered for any initiative.

The author dislikes the wording of that mantra, although the principle is great. "People Practices Things" are more general words. We will use these three concepts to look now at aspects of introducing Standard+Case. We start with People: the impact on culture, organisation, roles, responsibilities, training, careers and personal development.

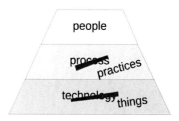

Knowledge Workers

The people we deal with most in S+C are knowledge workers. Davenport[2] defines them well:

> Knowledge workers have high degrees of expertise, education, or experience, and the primary purpose of their jobs involves the creation, distribution, or application of knowledge

They have important characteristics[3] we must deal with:

- Knowledge workers like autonomy – don't impinge on it.

- Specifying the detailed procedures is harder and less valuable – accept unstructured work.

- They need to be observed to be understood – be with them and review their work.

- They have good reasons for what they do – they are the experts on improving their work.

- Commitment matters – don't damage it.

- They value their knowledge as a personal asset and don't readily share.

---

[1] There are other more extended models such as "People Process Product Partners" and so on.

[2] T Davenport, *Thinking for a Living*. See bibliography

[3] Davenport again

It is not possible to learn everything about how a knowledge worker works by observation or measurement. They work in their heads. Nor is an external expert likely to be more expert than the person performing a knowledge-worker role. Knowledge workers know what they are doing better than anyone else and need to be allowed to do it.

Nothing is black and white between process workers and knowledge workers. There will always be process present in any role, and there will be opportunities to improve it with external expertise. A balance needs to be found between interventionist external process improvement and consultative facilitated knowledge-work improvement.

This book doesn't try to cover such human resource considerations as culture, organisational structure, physical facilities and co-location, remuneration and benefits, leadership and management, though clearly these are all important in getting top performance out of individually-empowered workers.

The results of knowledge work are notoriously difficult to quantify. In this book's specific domain of service response, there is a transactional nature and a focused outcome that makes it a little easier. We can look at numbers of responses and get some measures of how good the resolutions were, but only up to a point. For example a service desk can meet all numeric targets and still be universally loathed, do damage to the company, and lose or waste money.

Knowledge worker is a broad categorisation. Be careful not to treat all knowledge workers the same. It is useful to have a more finely grained understanding of the people responding. For example[1]:

> A new "eWorkforce" group at Intel, for example, has created one based primarily on mobility and behaviors and attitudes toward technology. Its categories are as follows:
>
> Functionalists: Primarily manufacturing (there are some office workers here, however) workers who use information technology occasionally, but do not rely heavily on "office IT" to perform their job functions
>
> Cube captains: Spend the majority of their time in the office, are very mainstream in their office IT needs, and are overall very happy with the tool sets they have
>
> Nomads: Heavy users of remote access; whether while traveling or working in remote offices, they need mobility in their IT environments
>
> Global collaborators: Interface often with people around the world; they have elements of the nomad segment, but they work across time zones and do a lot of collaboration and hence need access to collaboration tools anywhere, anytime
>
> Tech individualists: They want and need the latest IT tools and are willing to take risks with them; are also often early adopters

---

[1] Davenport again

Behaviour

Cultural changes are required to support Case Management. It takes years to really change the culture of an organisation, but we can make changes to the "climate": the outer, manifest environment in which people function.

Never tell people how to do things. Tell them what to do and they will surprise you with their ingenuity.
~ General George Patton.

For the adoption of Case Management, there needs to be
a climate of empowerment, trust, professionalism, valuing knowledge, respect for expertise, user-focus, and drive for outcomes.

After altering the climate comes modification of behaviour. Change the way people do things and eventually it will change the underlying culture - it will become accepted as 'the way we do things around here".

Make change happen[1]

Change is driven from a high level. It needs the commitment of the top executive. Without that it is much more difficult.

Change is an on-going programme, with no end.

Talk change over with those who will be affected by it, and those who will have to do it, and those who will have to pay for the effort.

If you have drummed up enthusiasm, get a small team together. Find one or two champions who will push it along. Also set up a steering group of bosses and experts to keep it on track.

Do the vision thing: define what you want to achieve and why, and come up with a concise way to say that. Then get the team doing some hard work selling the idea to everyone who will be affected.

Work out what might get in the way (including people), and how to overcome or remove obstacles.

Make people accountable and measure them. Improvement is hard unless a single person has ownership, and is answerable and empowered.

Find a few quick wins. Do something that shows good early results – nothing convinces sceptics better than results.

Don't invent stuff yourselves where you don't need to: draw from outside. This book lists some important resources: set one or two on your team to become your resident experts on Case

---

[1] This section was based on John Kotter's 8-step change model (ref 3)

Management theory. Also find external people who have done what you want to do before: talk it over; hire their experience if you need to.

Use early successes to build momentum. Progressively work up to bigger and better things. People accept evolution more readily than revolution.

Don't lose what you achieve. Get it embedded in the way things are done, in people's practices and habits, in the rules and the metrics and the policy of your organisation.

We cannot stress enough that any transformation of practices which ignores the people aspects will at best yield less than it could have, and at worst it will fail … sometimes spectacularly and sometimes slowly crumbling over time.

Changing people

People don't change on their own. They need motivation, communication and development.

Motivate them in these ways: by getting them involved and consulted; by showing how they benefit from the change; by making them accountable and measuring that accountability (with consequences); and by incenting them.

Communicate early, communicate often, and be as transparent about decision-making as you can. Tough decisions are more palatable if people understand why. Communication is two-way: consult, solicit feedback (including anonymous), run workshops and town-halls.

Development is not just one training course. Training should be followed up, refreshed, and repeated for new entrants. Training is not enough: practical workshops, on-the-job monitoring, coaching support, local super-users and many other mechanisms all help people learn what they need to make change successful.

Empowering the Customer

A major criticism of process-centric approaches like ITIL is that IT becomes inflexible, bureaucratic, unhelpful. Customers want to engage IT in a more creative mode than via formalised ITSM processes.

The customer (the business owner of the service, paying for it either directly or indirectly) doesn't expect to fill in forms to be talking about changes to a service. They want a discussion with an expert who has the flexibility to determine how to fulfil their needs and the initiative to generate the formal change processes for them. Put another way, one aspect of what ITIL calls Business Relationship Management can be considered as a case management interface to the back-office formal processes.

Empowering the Worker

Another criticism of process-centric approaches is that they don't empower the worker – in fact they shackle or constrain skilled people's ability to get the job done.

Standard+Case says that sufficiently skilled and experienced staff should be pre-approved to treat non-standard tickets as a case (to work out how to solve it based on the situation at hand), whilst providing them with:

- insight into the strategy they are contributing to

- good tools

- access to knowledge

- and clear policies and guidelines.

That's empowerment. By adopting a Case approach, we unleash the potential of our best knowledge workers by allowing them to adopt one of the most challenging roles in service response: the case worker.

Hero culture

The term "hero culture" refers to an undesirable situation where we depend on individual "heroes" to save us from negatively-impacting situations, and those heroes are rewarded for (a) hoarding their knowledge to build their own importance instead of sharing it to grow others and (b) fixing situations instead of preventing them – sometimes the situations are of their own making.

We must take care to ensure that recognising and empowering case workers does not reinforce such a culture. This requires a good emphasis on collaboration, coaching, and sharing of knowledge.

Transparency

Along with empowerment of case workers comes a requirement for transparency in decision-making about strategy, policy, architecture and other sets of rules.

If staff are given high levels of autonomy, they need to buy-in to the rules and bounds, to understand why they are there, what the rationale is. It is not enough to say "Thou shalt…" They need to understand the objectives, the intent. This motivates them to comply, and it allows them to understand where they can and cannot apply any discretion.

Employees will commit to a manager's decision – even one they disagree with – if they believe that the process the manager used to make the decision was fair[1]. There are three principles of **fair process**:

- **Engagement**. People need to feel involved and consulted in the decision-making process. They want to be heard.

- **Explanation**. People must understand why the decision was made the way it was. The decision process should be transparent.

- **Expectation clarity**. Once a decision is made, everyone should be clear on what that now means: what has changed; how things will be assessed differently. The new rules should be communicated.

Success

Staff members who are held accountable for the performance of some response process often feel frustrated by a small number of long-running tickets which make their results look bad. These are the tricky instances that are likely to be dealt with as cases, because they don't fit the standard models. We hope they will be dealt with more quickly as a result of being handled as a case: staff will be more successful when given a formalised approach and resources.

Even if responses are not resolved any quicker, management can intuitively recognise that cases are more likely to be long-running than standard responses: they will be seen less as a failure of the process.

In addition, each change of state for a case can be seen as progress whereas in a standard approach, it might be seen as "thrashing around" within a single Resolve step of the process which was "going nowhere".

As a result, management will have more visibility of the actual situation staff are dealing with – what proportion of responses are non-standard – and staff will feel more successful and less frustrated.

This applies to developing new systems as well as supporting existing ones. One practitioner described how their organisation had built a service request catalogue at considerable cost, only to find that by the time it was live, new request types had emerged, and even more request types came out of the woodwork that had been there all along yet they had not been formally recognised by analysis. The net result was a catalogue that covered only 60% of incoming requests.

This was seen as a failure of the design rather than a fact of life, because there is this common expectation that formalised process models should be able to cover all situations. S+C says that such an expectation simply isn't realistic: there will always be exceptions. We want exception cases to be perceived as "normal" rather than as failures in response process or system design.

---

[1] *Fair Process: Managing in the Knowledge Economy*, W. C. Kim and R. A. Mauborgne, Harvard Business Review 1997

Utilisation

There needs to be a level of slack staff capacity to respond, like fire-fighters. Few service desks today are working on developing slack capacity: they are all increasing efficiency and squeezing numbers. This denies the reality that many situations are complex and unpredictable. With too much emphasis on efficiency and not enough on effectiveness, the function gets broken. We cut all the fat and start on muscle.

The Lean methodology recognises three forms of waste: muda (futility) mura (unevenness) and muri (overburdened), but you wouldn't know it to see most Lean initiatives, which are all about eliminating muda; unnecessary work, idleness. As the Wikipedia entry for muda[1] says

> Muda has been given much greater attention as waste than the other two which means that whilst many Lean practitioners have learned to see muda they fail to see in the same prominence the wastes of mura and muri

Good Lean practitioners understand the Theory of Constraints: that the fastest path is limited by (usually) one governing constraint or bottleneck. Relieving that constraint will increase efficiency. Relieving any other apparent constraint will have no effect. Maximum efficiency of case workers doesn't come from maximum utilisation: it comes from having a sufficient workforce to deal with cases as they come in so that the case is resolved as quickly as possible.

Standard responses are transactional. You may be able to optimise the system to maximise utilisation of Standard workers. Case response are not transactional, they are unpredictable. You cannot adjust the system to maximise case worker utilisation: you need to adjust the system to maximise handling of cases. Put simply, this will mean case workers sitting around sometimes, like firemen. Like firemen, you can put them to work maintaining and improving their methods, skills, and resources.

Accreditation

Case workers are given more autonomy and discretion than most response staff. It is important that people have sufficient skills, knowledge and experience to manage cases with maximum effectiveness and minimum risk.

One way to assure this is to require case workers to be accredited for the role.

There is no independent certification (testing) or accreditation (professional recognition) of case workers except in specific industry sectors.

For example the author was keen to become a Certified Case Manager (CCM®) until I discovered I first needed to gain accreditation in the USA as a nurse. There is no certification of case managers in the IT sector.

---

[1] http://en.wikipedia.org/wiki/Muda_(Japanese_term)

So employers will need to identify industry-specific certifications or create an in-house testing regime. In the IT sector, the ITIL Operational Support and Analysis (OSA) Intermediate certification[1] is probably the closest thing, but it tests only theoretical knowledge of ITIL processes, not any of the other knowledge or techniques of case management.

In addition to theoretical certification, accreditation considers the individual's capability, track record, practical skills and experience.

Once again there is no relevant independent IT accreditation. An ITIL Master certification might be suitable but it is likely to be overly complex and arduous for a response case worker.

This leaves in-house accreditation. One option is to combine a core theoretical certification like ITIL's OSA with other criteria related to internal certifications (see "Gamification" below) and required levels of experience.

Another approach is to simply recognise the most senior staff available. This is expedient but misleading. Seniority and experience are not direct measures of capability to be a case worker. They contribute to the level of knowledge and skill, but seniority should not itself be the sole measure of accreditation. Accrediting case workers forces us to face up to an issue that is often ignored in IT organisations: seniority isn't enough; we need to directly measure and certify people's capability.

How many training course have you been to where everyone got a prize ("passed" the course) just by turning up – there was no exam? This is a peculiar aspect of corporate training in general and IT training in particular. Even when there is examination, the tutor is often assessed on the pass-rate and yet operates unsupervised – which almost guarantees ethical boundaries will be explored in coaching the students to the exam rather than the topic.

Allowing someone to practice as a case worker is a high risk decision, for the individual as well as the organisation. We discuss the importance of providing clear policy for the protection of both parties. It is also important that we equip the individual with adequate resources, and sufficient skills and knowledge. The only way we can know that they have sufficient skills and knowledge is to test and accredit them.

---

[1] http://www.itil-officialsite.com/Qualifications/ITILQualificationLevels/OperationalSupportandAnalysis.aspx

Stratification

Some cultures are uncomfortable with stratification of the workforce, but Case Management makes it essential. Staff need to accept that they haven't yet learnt enough to be a case worker; or that they don't have the capabilities and never will. It is OK to give everybody the opportunity to try, to prove their ability, but this must be on a trial basis, once again for the protection of both parties.

Graves[1] has an interesting model of certification which can be related to the Cynefin model[2]:

Trainee	Simple	10-100 hours	"follow the instructions…"
Apprentice	Complicated	100-1000 hours	"learn the theory"
Journeyman	Complex	1000-10,000 hours	"it depends…"
Expert	Chaotic	10,000+ hours	"nothing is certain…"

He suggests the following training that each level would be certified against[3]:

Trainee   Work instructions; application of work-instructions in live practice; how to identify when to escalate to someone with greater experience.

Apprentice   Shared terminology; theory behind work-instructions (various levels of theory); links between theory and practice; reasoning from the particular to the general.

Journeyman   Complexity, ambiguity, uncertainty, probability, possibility; adaptation from the general to the particular (context-specific).

Master   Practical application in unique contexts, in multiple and often interleaving (recursive) timescales.

---

[1] http://weblog.tetradian.com/2013/01/28/over-certainties-of-certification/

[2] Graves would be unhappy about me doing that, as he strongly differentiates his own SCAN model from Cynefin. It is done to avoid introducing yet another model to this book.

[3] See Graves' article for recommendations on how to test each level for certification.

Gamification

Service desks have always struggled to offer challenges and a growth path to professional service desk analysts (those who want to make a career on the service desk rather than seeing it as a stepping-stone to somewhere – anywhere – else).

Gamification is a cool new solution to that issue. It also has potential for other teams: Level 2 and 3 Support, IT Operations, Development, DevOps, and so on.

Gamification is the application of ideas and principles from online gaming (yes: World of Warcraft, MineCraft, Call of Duty, that kind of thing) to other contexts, especially at work. Gamification motivates and encourages workers by making their tasks more engaging, by rewarding desired behaviours, by giving them a path to recognition and status, and by introducing an element of fun.

Gamification challenges and stretches people, and it recognises their achievements and experience. Standard+Case fits well with gamification to support a growth path for service desk professionals:

- Rank the Standard models by difficulty in executing them.

- Make training in each model available to service desk analysts, e.g. online courses.

- Give staff a badge for being certified for a model (gamification). This badge can appear in any context alongside their name, such as their digital persona on the ticketing tool, staff directory, email, collaboration tools and so on. Badges can even be placed on their name-plates on their cubicles or desks.

- For some Standard models, there will be a preference that they be executed by a certified staff member and work will get allocated that way; for other Standard models the staff member *must* be certified (e.g. sensitive data).

- Only the most senior, SM-Case-certified staff members (those who have "levelled up": gamification) get to do Case Management, to deal with non-standard tickets.

A hypothetical "gamified" service desk tool.

Career in Response

Standard+Case improves job satisfaction for service desk analysts, especially those in the role with intent to stay as a professional. With S+C, the service desk analyst is not faced with the prospect of resetting passwords or adding people to security groups for the rest of their lives: they know they can grow to get first access to more challenging work. And the new guy doesn't get tossed into the deep end of coordinating techs and knowledge to resolve tricky cases: they are put onto the simpler standard models until they can learn.

Standard+Case provides a clear path of increasing seniority based on knowledge and skills – whether you wrap it in gamification or not. It rewards and recognises the most expert staff by "letting them loose" on Case Management as empowered case workers.

Personal brand

For an individual to be a case worker, they need to be perceived as having authority and expertise. They must inspire confidence. This means paying attention to their brand: their personal image, their network, their peer group, their followers, and especially to the value they provide to other team members, internal and external. This value can come from:

- knowledge shared (the top priority)

- advice and support provided

- mentoring or coaching

- resources contributed, shared or loaned

Development

Building a team or teams of expert case workers requires investment and commitment from the organisation in their individual development, and high levels of personal ownership by the individuals of their own professional development. Both parties - the employer and the employee - can be expected to invest in the skills and resources of the modern knowledge worker.

Staff that deal with responses will need new or increased skills in several disciplines to be case workers. Often overlooked is the need for the basic skills in written and oral communication, presentation skills, networking, collaboration, management and delegation, facilitation of meetings and workshops, time and priority management, the organisation's administrative systems, personal knowledge management, personal computing, business writing (proposals, business cases, reports…) and other skills that become more important with increased autonomy and responsibility.

Much of this can be taught but ultimately there is no substitute for on-the-job learning through experience.

So an important element of development is to provide people with opportunities to grow. This can be done by assigning them lower risk cases where they have room to fail, or better still by partnering case workers of different seniority levels. There is a good reason why every cop movie or series features two partners: a wise senior one and a struggling junior one. Coaching, apprenticeship, and mentoring schemes are all important in knowledge transfer from existing case workers to trainees.

Project management

Case responses are unlikely to be structured as formal projects, but some of the skills of project management are important because many cases will be complex enough that they will benefit from being managed with some level for formality drawn from the project management discipline:

- planning, assessing plans, and re-planning
- estimating
- building and assessing business cases
- understanding organisational value and imperatives
- managing risk
- getting to an outcome; the ability to deliver
- quality management; benefits realisation
- assessing viability, and the probability of success
- requisitioning and mobilising resources
- tracking and reporting progress
- delegation, and managing by exception
- managing up: including buffering the practitioners from concerned senior managers
- working to a budget

Negotiation and mediation

Closely linked to the project management skillset is the ability to negotiate agreements and mediate disagreements including skills for:

- understanding politics, and authority structures
- listening, interviewing, fact-finding
- developing buy-in
- finding win-win outcomes
- gaining consensus

Human support

In the extreme or exceptional situations that are dealt with as cases, the user/client is more likely to be stressed or upset, and the impacts on them personally are more likely to be negative.

Inter-personal skills become even more important: the case worker is called on to be supportive of the client as a person.

"People do not care how much you know until they know how much you care."

- John Maxwell

Case managers are skilled in applying psychology to interactions with users. The following principles have proven to be effective[1]. Train your staff in them:

- Get bad experiences over with early: talk about the difficult bits first. Communicate empathy for the client's plight.

- Break up pleasure and combine pain: bring all the unpleasant bits together. Sprinkle the good news throughout the discussion.

- Finish strongly: have a positive (scripted?) finish, emphasising the benefits to the user.

- Give users choice: allow them to be in control as much as possible. Steer them but give them their rights.

- Let users stick to their habits. Don't force change unless absolutely necessary. If the old way is good enough, leave it alone. When they must change, ease them across gradually.

Empowering the User

We need users (the end consumers of the services) to engage with IT via the formalised interface of request management, so that we have tracking, control, prioritisation, load management and so on. In most organisations, we can't have users engaging our case workers directly, else they would be overwhelmed.

But we all know the user's frustrations of having to work our way through the low-level process 'factory' workers to 'prove' we have a non-Standard request or incident, so we can eventually get access to an expert.

One solution is indeed **to handle everything with case workers** if we can afford to (see "Case+Standard").

Another alternative is to **expose the Standard models to users**, perhaps through a software "wizard" or a decision tree. Allow the users to determine the model and initiate the workflow. Allow the users to determine that no Standard model fits and a case worker is required.

---

1   *Using behavioural science to improve the customer experience*, J DeVine, K Gilson, McKinsey Quarterly 2010 http://hbswk.hbs.edu/item/6201.html

A third option is to **certify users, possibly using gamification**. Users can "prove" their technical ability to self-diagnose. This could be automatic because of their role in the company; from membership in certain external organisations such as computer societies; from external qualifications/accreditations such as Cisco or Microsoft certifications, IT certified professionals, or ITIL Experts; it could come through an online reputational index such as Quora or LinkedIn endorsements; or they may need to sit a test.

Just ass response staff can level up to higher expertise and operate as case workers, so too users can certify as expert users, who are allowed to enter the system when they determine their need is non-standard by going direct to a case worker. That case worker may gate them back to a lower-expertise worker to follow a standard-model, but only after determining that it is what they need. The case worker knows the certified user will have done some self-diagnosis and is likely to be selecting the correct option on entry.

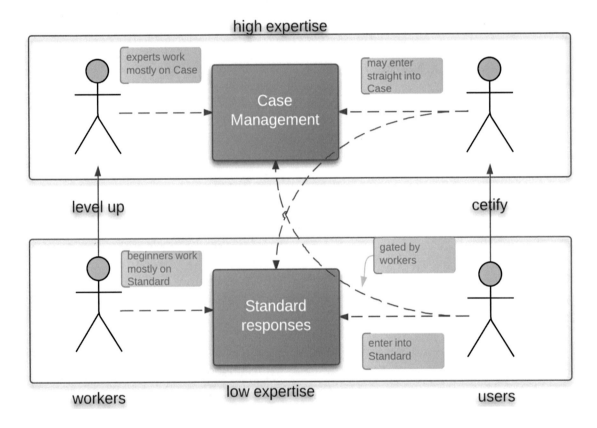

Practices

The second of the three aspects – "People Practices Things" – is Practices, often called process, though that is a sloppy use of the word. A process is a formal activity with defined inputs and outputs. A practice is the broader discipline, including policy, plans, roles, responsibilities, teams, functions, tools, templates, techniques, procedures, work instructions ... and processes.

Standard+Case is not a set of practices; it is an expanded way of doing existing practices if those practices involve humans responding to situations.

Process

Recall that we spoke of a generic ticketing and handling process for responses of any sort:

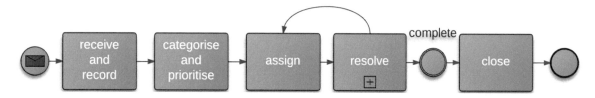

Standard+Case doesn't abandon this generic process. In general, the only part of the process that S+C will alter is the Resolve step:

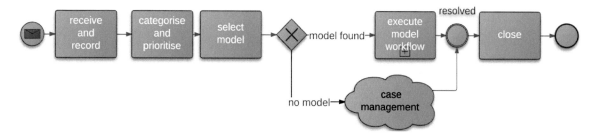

See the point where the process branches: is there a standard model for responding to this ticket? If yes, then it is a Standard ticket. If no, then we need to use Case Management to resolve it. That simple decision point is the core of Standard+Case.

Standard+Case process has little or no process for the Resolve step for Case tickets (hence a fuzzy cloud in the diagram, not a process box), and otherwise *the process is unchanged*.

There are any number of procedures we can use as resources and assemble as needed during Resolve. Some of those procedures one might glorify with the title of "sub-process" but that is not a good term when there is no parent process. There is no parent process for the Resolve step. The case changes state in response to information uncovered and external events, and actions taken. This is unpredictable.

That's the whole point of Case: there is no process but it can still be highly structured and controlled. We get locked into the thinking in IT that process provides controls. Standardised process is only one way to control activity, and it doesn't work in unknown or unfamiliar situations. One can argue after a case is completed that there *was* a process – one can see the steps that were executed – but one cannot predict in advance what that process will be, or even what all the possible process paths will be. And it will differ from case to case. S+C is not a new way of working: knowledge workers already resort to case management to deal with "hard" tickets, without calling it that. But S+C formalises the non-process-driven "exceptions" into a Case methodology and defines rules around their handling: who, what, and when. We treat Case as normal, not an exception condition.

Categorise

In the Categorise And Prioritise step of the process above, there is a diagnosis activity to determine enough information to be able to categorise the ticket. The diagnosis will either identify a matching standard model, or the situation will be categorised as **unfamiliar or non-standard** – we know what is happening but we do not have a standard model for it. If it is the latter, this will be treated as a case.

At some point there needs to be a cut-off mechanism in diagnosis – a gating point – to decide that the ticket cannot be categorised, that it is **unknown** – i.e. the category cannot (yet) be determined. This should also be treated as a case.

One of the first activities of dealing with a case will be investigation, i.e. further information gathering and deeper diagnosis. It is possible that such investigation will uncover enough information to suggest that this is a Standard situation after all – that we may have a model procedure to deal with it – so the process diagram can be amended to show this with a loop back to selecting a model.

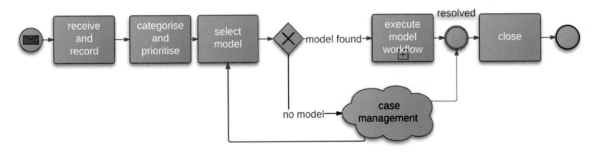

Measurement

Much ITSM measurement of response practices is distorted by unwittingly mixing standard and case situations in the same data. We get long-running tickets (e.g. incidents or problems) that frustrate everyone and make the process statistics look bad, when in fact they have fallen outside the standard process.

Those long-running tickets should not be reported against service level targets that were designed for measuring only standardised process. We should have separate service level targets for Case. For example, you cannot have target resolution times for unpredictable scenarios. Imagine the police having target resolution times for cold cases. (See "Service Levels").

As Davenport puts it[1]:

> There is no Frederick Taylor equivalent for knowledge work. As a result we lack measures, methods, and rules of thumb for improvement... With no clear alternative to Taylorist approaches, however, there may be attempts to apply those approaches to knowledge work.

Cases cannot be measured merely by the counting of anything. It is the quality of the work that matters, i.e. the effectiveness. For example, the number of cases handled per month clearly does not relate at all to customer satisfaction with the service.

The primary mean of understanding and improving case management is not statistical measurement. We derive our most important learning from reviewing individual cases (see "Review and Improve").

However statistical measurement does provide secondary benefits, giving us a dashboard to the overall health of the system and possibly identifying trends and problems. With a large enough population, unpredictable events do form predictable distributions.

The most important measures are the inputs (demand) and the outputs (efficiency and effectiveness).

The starting point to understanding how to improve Case Management is to understand what the customer demand is, i.e. what the system is required to do. (More of this in "Adopting Standard+Case" but for now we need to understand the measurements that can contribute to that understanding.)

Categorisation of cases is important in order to develop statistics about the patterns of demand, but the issue is that at first all cases will be unknown (not enough information to categorise) or unfamiliar (not an existing category), so categorisation should happen as part of the Close step in the response, and we should only measure information about closed responses, not while they are still open.

---

[1] *Thinking for a Living.* See bibliography.

Measurement of inputs might include:

- volume of response requests

- percentage of responses that are standard

- breakdown of responses by category

- breakdown of responses by user demographics – where are they coming from?

- number of new standard categories identified – how fast is the world changing?

There is still a place for "industrial" performance measures in Case Management, measuring the outputs. We need to monitor efficiency and effectiveness, and we can further divide effectiveness into quality and compliance.

Some performance metrics that could be applied to Case Management to measure **efficiency** include:

- percentage of cases resolved

- backlog of cases

- cumulative costs for Case Management (against budget if there is one) and average cost per case

- resource usage, e.g. Full Time Equivalent (FTE) or person-hours

- average number of states per case, and variance

- average time per state

  We can't control how many states a case goes through (and therefore we can't control how long the overall resolution takes) but we can try to reduce the time spent in each state.

- average time to resolve, and variance

  Even though in theory we cannot predict the number of states a case goes through, we know intuitively that a decreasing average resolution time will be an indicator of doing something right. This is not the same thing as the number of outlier cases outside some target time – we should focus on the successful through-put not the slow outliers. In unpredictable situations, individual instances that take a long time are not an indicator of something going wrong. We can and should study outliers for learnings, but statistically measuring them is less useful.

- number of new Standard Models created

- volume of knowledge produced

- percentage of cold cases

Quality metrics will often be specific to the organisation but some general ones include:

- customer and partner satisfaction with case handling

- number of rejections of output documents and other products

- grading the effectiveness of the response during Review

- quality of knowledge produced, measured by feedback mechanisms and usage

- cost/impact to the business of long running cases: we can't always resolve these but we must do something to contain the impact

We should also measure **compliance** with policy, which should include any standards and rules. So we could measure:

- percentage of responses that were incorrectly classified as cases

- completeness of checklists for mandatory inputs, tasks, and/or outputs

- average degree of compliance to standards criteria for reviewed cases

- average degree of compliance to policy rules for reviewed cases

Of course some of these metrics can also be broken down by team and for individual case workers.

Finally, we need to measure the usefulness of our **tools** and other resources. We can measure:

- how often a tool, knowledge item or other resource was used

- time spent using a tool

- +1 / -1 from the case worker on the usefulness of a resource

Cases are hard to measure. This is not a problem introduced by S+C. It is a problem we already have. S+C recognises the problem, formalises it, and gives us structures to start measuring cases better.

Maturity

There is a fixation with maturity of processes in service management, certainly in ITSM.

Every organisation does nearly every practice there is in service management. It is how well they do them and manage them that vary. Maturity assessments often look at how well a practice/process is **managed**, on the assumption that well-managed processes are more readily improved.

Most process-management maturity scales use something like the following levels of maturity:

None	There is no detectible trace of the practice
Ad-hoc	Chaotic. It is done but with no consistency. How it happens depends on who does it and other circumstances
Consistent	A repeatable process. It happens much the same way every time: for the same initial conditions it gives the same result.
Defined	The practice is documented and official, and staff are trained in it – it is passed on as people come and go.

| Managed | Someone is in charge of it. We can see how well we are doing – we get metrics. |
| Improved | We track how we are doing and work to make it better (up to some point of diminishing returns) |

Remember, assessments like this measure how well you **manage.** They don't measure how well you **execute** the service, only how *equipped* you are to improve. To assess how well you actually *do* your practices, you must first have:

(1) a reference model of the "best practice" for your job or industry (known as a PAM or Process Assessment Model) and

(2) an instrument: a questionnaire or other tool for measuring consistently.

For a framework and method for measuring maturity of *execution* of practices, see ISO/IEC 15504 (a.k.a. SPICE) which has a strong IT flavour but is actually applicable to assess any practice, if you have a PAM and a measurement instrument.

Whether measuring management or execution, a Case Management approach would score less for the Resolve step, because of its lack of defined structured process for the step. Note however that S+C uses the existing processes for all other steps, with standard Resolve processes for known categories, meaning that the maturity of the overall response process from end to end can be just as high as for a fully standardised process.

A non-process-oriented way of measuring maturity of execution is required for the Case Management activity in the Resolve step. One possible avenue for assessing Case Management maturity is by looking at the defined states and the tools/techniques for a given value stream[1].

0	Absent
1	Ad-hoc state definitions, tools/techniques applied
2	Generally accepted toolsets and state definitions within subdomains that differ across the overall organisation
3	A common set of state definitions, tools, techniques, and guidelines are in force across the overall organisation
4	Case states and transitions are tied back to organisational value and integrated into service offerings
5	Case Management practice is continually improved and treated as a strategic asset by the organisation

We do not yet have a PAM for SM-case, but there is a maturity model for the use of software to support Case Management. See "Things".

---

[1] This model was proposed by Roger Williams when reviewing this book.

Collaboration

Case Management is inherently more of a collaborative practice than Standard models are. Standard process transfers or "escalates" ownership of discrete tasks more than emphasising collaboration. This is part of the broader evolution towards the knowledge-worker organisation. Case requires support for collaboration within teams that cross the organisational boundary. The support must facilitate collaboration as well as recording all the resulting communications for later review and audit.

We can look again at the Cynefin model, from the perspective of the social networks within each situation type[1].

We tend to find decentralised networks in all states but Simple. The Simple situation tends to suit a hierarchal "star" network: central management of workers working on assigned tasks, i.e. the standardised approach.

The Complicated situations tend to have central orchestration as well as local networks, whereas the Complex is typified by multiple networks of workers coming together to explore and develop ideas.

In the Chaotic situation such as an emergency, networks are loosely coupled trying to gain control and move it into another state.

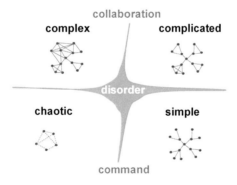

So in situations that are unfamiliar or unknown we need to reduce the central command and control, and allow workers to decentralise and collaborate locally using Case Management. In situations that are known we can take central control and use Standard responses, and in situations that are chaotic we try to find control.

---

[1] *Managing Structured and Unstructured Processes Under the Same Umbrella*, A.Manuel, in *How Knowledge Workers Get Things Done*, p88

Case Process

For the process aficionados who simply cannot bear the concept that there is no process in Case Management, we can map out a general sequence of steps that will probably occur for each state of the case – a sub-process for the Resolve step.

1. Investigate:

    - Have we resolved the case? What do we know? What don't we know?

2. Determine the state:

    - Diagnose / deduce.

    - Define what the state is.

    - Identify whether it could be a standard model after all.

3. Determine options:

    - What state could we get to and how? What do we need? What must we produce?

4. Decide goals and actions, also known as an agenda, a checklist of tasks.

5. Deploy resources.

6. Act.

7. Repeat until resolved or cold.

We need to re-iterate here that the case worker is not bound to this sub-process for case resolution, nor are they measured on compliance with it.

It looks something like this, although the BPM paradigm is getting a little stretched here:

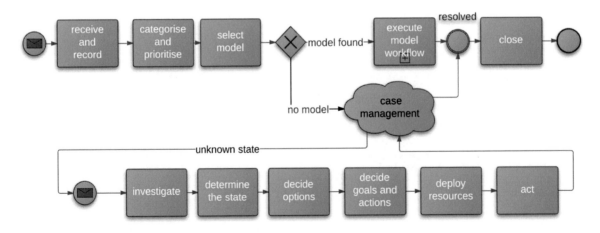

Methods

Kanban[1]

Originating from Lean methodologies, Kanban (Japanese for "visual map") can be used as a practical instrument for processing cases. Kanban can refer to:

- the Kanban board, a physical board which enables process management (what, when, how much)

- the Kanban method, a method for process change in organisations

The Kanban method is based on 6 core practices:

- visualisation

- limit Work in Progress (WIP) via a pull system

- manage flow

- explicit policies

- feedback loops

- incremental improvements

Kanban essentially serves as a signalling system, available to a specific team, facilitating the resolution of a variety of tasks. Usually small, standard, repetitive and short tasks are not handled via the Kanban system, this is usually too inefficient. It is much more suitable for managing, monitoring and resolving cases. An increasing number of organisations have started using Kanban to track incidents, changes, problems and releases. In addition, Kanban is used more and more as the organisation's CSI engine, visualizing the realisation flows for service and process improvements.

As an alternative, Kanban may be mixed with Scrum practices, resulting in ScrumBan boards. Roughly, these are Kanban boards equipped to include sprints (cycles of work). This may be useful in dealing with releases, which need to follow the organisation's drumbeat.

Kanban combines the simple concept that Work In Progress (WIP) should be limited to some maximum capacity with an equally simple visual tool of cards stuck on a wall (actual or virtual). Kanban throttles throughput to a maximum number of cards in each space, in order to increase efficiency and effectiveness. Kanban improves throughput, focuses behaviour and encourages collaboration. It also exposes bottlenecks.

A full description of Kanban is beyond the scope of this book but it is clearly an excellent mechanism for managing the Case workload. There are a few reservations: Kanban comes from a manufacturing background and does try to reduce variability and standardise tasks, so there will be a tension with some Kanban concepts and techniques, and some of them will be simply

---

[1] Thanks to Dave van Herpen for contributing to this section. For more information see Wikipedia http://en.wikipedia.org/wiki/Kanban_(development)

unsuitable for Case Management. But the basic principles of controlling the level of WIP and deciding the priority of waiting cases are useful so long as Kanban accepts that there is no predefined sequence of steps for a case, nor can the time be predicted.

Kanban is already in use for managing workload within traditional response teams doing Standard work. Case could be added to a Kanban board as another swimlane, or the case workers could have the own board and exchange cards with the Standard response group(s). There will likely only be four columns in the Case swimlane: "to do", "next", "working on it", and "done": cases can't have any other predictable intermediate states. There could be multiple swimlanes for different types of cases, relating to different teams of caseworkers. The point is to manage workload for a given set of case workers.

Here is a sample of how it might be laid out:

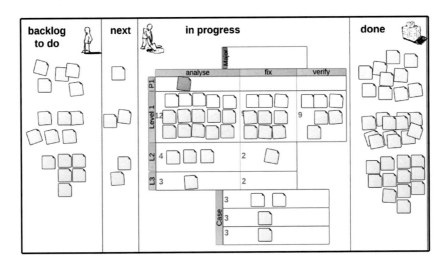

Knowledge Centered Support

Knowledge Centered Support[1] is very useful for case management. KCS[SM] is[2]

> a set of practices for creating and maintaining knowledge in a support environment. Unlike the traditional add-on process of knowledge engineering, KCS is an integral part of day-to-day operation in support centers. KCS becomes the way people solve problems and creates knowledge as a by-product of problem solving.

> While KCS is enabled by technology, KCS is primarily about people. People are the source of knowledge. KCS has proven that the best people to capture and maintain support knowledge are the people who create and use it every day – the support analysts.

---

[1] http://www.serviceinnovation.org/kcs/

[2] KCS Academy http://www.thekcsacademy.net/kcs/

For optimum performance, KCS practices and the tools that support them must be integrated with other support and business systems, including incident management, change management, and service level management processes and systems.

KCS^{SM} has four basic concepts:

- Integrate the creation and maintenance of knowledge into the problem solving process.

- Evolve content based on demand and usage.

- Develop a knowledge base of collective experience to date.

- Reward learning, collaboration, sharing, and improving.

The principles of KCS are very similar to those of Case: knowledge at the centre; capturing, improving, and eventually packaging and publishing selected knowledge.

KCS provides clever ideas for improving knowledge, including:

- measure the usage of knowledge articles

- allow staff and users to rate knowledge articles

- bubble-up best knowledge articles, based on ratings and the frequency of use

- allow staff and users to flag knowledge articles for review

- promote best staff knowledge articles into published user articles ("Level Zero Support", user self-service)

- make knowledge contribution everybody's job

- reward sharing not knowing

Knowledge sharing

Knowledge Centered Support is an advanced example of a knowledge sharing method. Others include:

- **Team meetings**. Don't underestimate the value of getting groups together on a regular basis to share what they have been doing and what they learned. Encourage all attendees to come with something to share at every meeting (ritual humiliation for those who don't works).

- **Training**. Formal training from external sources has an important role in the introduction of knowledge, but equally important is the sharing of knowledge within the organisation through staff training others. This can be formal and large scale or informal and simple: discussion groups, webinars, "ignites" (in an "ignite" a speaker has a fixed time to speak to their set of slides that auto-advance).

- **Peer review and support**. Involve peers at important stages and decision points in cases.

- **Coaching and mentoring**. We don't do enough of these two activities in IT (no, they are not the same thing). Formal and informal practices should be developed, supported, and encouraged to allow senior staff to pass on their knowledge to their juniors.

- **Knowledge repositories**. IT as an industry struggles with developing good effective repositories of knowledge. They require large investment and solid commitment; a designated custodian[1]; and an effective system (plan, roles, procedures, reporting) to protect, maintain, and improve the repository.

The Confluence Sense-making Framework

The Confluence Sense-making Framework (CSF)[2] is a tool that a team uses to make sense of any situation in order to make decisions about it.

CSF uses a series of questions and a collaborative workshop approach to answering them in order to structure and analyse what we know about a situation.

It is a special way of thinking: it builds and then maps a landscape, looking for structures and states that are similar to the Cynefin model.

Root Cause Analysis

Root Cause Analysis is an activity that identifies the underlying or original cause of an incident or problem[3]. Root Cause Analysis is fundamental to Case Management. Root Cause Analysis techniques include:

- Barrier Analysis[4]: analyse the presence, absence, or level of use of physical or administrative barriers that should have alleviated or mitigated the problem

- Ishikawa Diagrams[5]: cause-and-effect or "fishbone" diagrams that deconstruct and group the causes of an event

- Kepner-Tregoe[6]: K-T Problem Analysis provides a process to identify and sort all the issues surrounding a decision[7]

---

[1] There is a school of thought that "everybody is responsible for knowledge" and a custodian is not required – in fact having one allows everybody else to not care. I view this as idealistic and impractical. There are ways to develop a culture of valuing knowledge: having an unkempt repository is not one of them.

[2] http://www.storycoloredglasses.com/p/confluence-sensemaking-framework.html

[3] *ITIL Glossary of Terms, Definitions and Acronyms V3*, 30 May 2007

[4] *USMBOK, Guide to the Universal Service Management Body of Knowledge*, Ian Clayton, Service Management 101; 2012, ISBN-13: 978-0981469102

[5] Ishikawa, Kaoru (Translator: J. H. Loftus); *Introduction to Quality Control*; 1990; ISBN 4-906224-61-X

[6] *The Rational Manager: A Systematic Approach to Problem Solving and Decision-Making*, C.H. Kepner, B.B. Tregoe; McGraw-Hill 1965; ISBN-13: 978-0070341753

[7] *Thinking About Problems: Kepner-Tregoe®*, H Marquis, DITY May 2010
http://www.itsmsolutions.com/newsletters/DITYvol6iss19.htm

- Service Failure Analysis: an activity that identifies underlying causes of one or more service interruptions. SFA identifies opportunities to improve the processes and tools, and not just the infrastructure. SFA is a time constrained, project-like activity, rather than an on-going process of analysis[1]

Some (including this author) argue that there is no single root cause of problems. It generally takes several causes together to create a problem – they have to "line up" in some way. Watch documentaries such as *Aircrash Investigation* to learn this over and over. By "root", people often mean the biggest cause or the primary focus for correction.

The first and most obvious cause you find is seldom the end of the story: keep asking "why" until the answers are not useful.

Complex systems are in fact permanently broken, so when they actually fail it is often nobody's fault.[2] The primary purpose of Root Cause Analysis during response or "post mortem" reviews after response is to prevent recurrence, not to assign blame. Make this explicit in any brief or instructions or introduction to the session. On the other hand there could be negligence. If this is worse than an honest human mistake, then it needs to be addressed, but do it with care and discretion: future reviews will not go well if staff think they are blame-seeking "witch hunts".

Brainstorming

The Confluence Sense-making Framework and Root Cause analysis are examples of brainstorming.

The principles of brainstorming were laid out by Osborn before the Second World War[3]. These include:

- aim for quantity

- withhold judgment or criticism

- reduce social inhibitions among group members

- stimulate idea generation

- welcome unusual or lateral ideas, embrace diversity

- combine and improve ideas

There are a number of general workshop brainstorming techniques for finding answers to situations or problems or questions, such as:

- Six Thinking Hats, De Bono's well known approach.

---

[1] *ITIL Glossary of Terms, Definitions and Acronyms V3*, 30 May 2007

[2] *How Complex Systems Fail*, Richard I. Cook, MD
http://www.ctlab.org/documents/How%20Complex%20Systems%20Fail.pdf

[3] *Applied Imagination: Principles and Procedures of Creative Problem-Solving*, A F Osborn, Scribner 3rd Ed. 1963, no ISBN

- 6-3-5 Brain-writing: 6 participants sit in a group; each participant thinks up 3 ideas every 5 minutes.

- Slip Writing. Gather ideas on paper or sticky notes, not spoken.

- Affinity diagram or KJ Method. Sorting ideas into related groups and subgroups.

- Stepladder Technique. Members join the group progressively one at a time.

- Reverse Brainstorming. Consider the opposite question or problem.

- Role-plays and walk-throughs. Consider the implications - how ideas might work.

Incident resources

Standard+Case can use existing resources from the service management practices of Incident Management, Major Incident Management and Business Continuity Management[1], such as:

- incident matching and other diagnostic techniques

- support knowledgebase

- communications plan

- business impact analysis and risk assessments

- escalation paths (contact details) and procedures

- procedures for raising problems, requests for change, work requests etc.

- procedure for forming a resolver team

- procedure for establishing a war-room / centre of operations

- technical intervention procedures, e.g. server re-boot, server re-build, recover a database

- supplier/partner support interlock, e.g. running a teleconference

- procedure for post-incident review

- ticket status and statistical reporting

- ticket auditing

Close

In industry sectors where the cases involve people, the case will generally only close if the subject dies or the case is resolved. With murder cases the case stays open even after the subject is dead! In theory police never close cold cases. How do we deal with SM cases? One can argue that we need a mechanism to abandon service cases; else we will not trigger the review where we can capture the learnings from the case (recall that review of individual tickets is more important in

---

[1] Major Incident Management and Continuity Management are both about Case Management. Both of them lay down policy, information, and tools for unpredictable situations.

Case than in Standard tickets because we get less meaningful statistical information with Case). An abandonment mechanism would primarily consist of:

- policy on closure

- an approval procedure

If there is distaste for closing cases, then an alternative is to have a mechanism to trigger a review for cold cases: those that are still open but appear to be unresolvable.

Review and Improve

Drive the review process for Case responses much harder than for Standard ones. We must commit to doing reviews of individual cases in Standard+Case: perhaps selected cases, perhaps all of them, as resource and policy dictate. IT as an industry sector has a reputation for being poor at actually performing adequate levels of review of responses. I bet everyone reading this doesn't do as much reviewing of standard tickets as you aspire to. You cannot afford to be that way with Case: reviews are our source of data, much more than stats. We need reviews for Case practice improvement, and for capturing new Standard models. If Case reviews happen, then the Case approach and all its subsidiary techniques, tools and resources can be improved over time. Issues identified by review would be fed into existing improvement systems. The Review step is essential to successful Case Management.

Improvement to S+C is integral to the approach. The Review process generates continual incremental improvement generated by the case workers and their reviewers.

Emphasise that reviews are mainly for learning and only secondarily for QA. Perform "blameless post mortems". (Although we may identify "learning opportunities" where the case could have been handled better, or should have been categorised as Standard, or other feedback for the case worker and others.)

Function

Reviews require a reviewing practice to be in place: a functional team who manage and perform reviews, a review policy, RACI charts, procedures, metrics, goals and KPIs, reporting, tools.

There are many mechanisms for reviewing activities. Consider:

- an expert inspector, e.g. the most senior case worker

- a peer jury – a group of case workers

- an external assessor, e.g. a hired consultant

- a management board – a panel of stakeholders

Each has its strengths and weaknesses. The choice will depend on the culture and politics of your organisation.

Selection

There are at least three key criteria for choosing which cases to review:

First, outliers in the metrics are not a good measure for judging Case Management execution performance because cases can be out of our control, but they are of great interest for improvement. In other words, don't beat people up because cases show a wide variation of metrics – cases are not standardised and should not be expected to be consistent. We should however choose the outliers for review because they are the most interesting; the cases that:

- closed very quickly or very slowly

- never closed

- had high or low quality of outputs

- had a very small or very large number of states

- cost a lot or a little

Secondly, find a way to flag cases that were resolved differently, however "different" may be defined. They may reveal better ways of dealing with situations. Diversity is our friend.

Finally, look for repeating situations, so that the process of resolving them can potentially be standardised, if it lends itself to standardisation. Recall the S+C criteria for standardisation are:

- acceptably low risk

- repeatable

- fully documented and tested

- unambiguously defined

Outputs

Reviews assess:

- how well policy was followed

- how good the outputs were

- how complete the records are

- what inputs were used

- what inputs were needed but unavailable

- what actions were taken in each state

- what was novel

- emerging trends and patterns

For a public domain method for continual service improvement, see the author's site http://www.basicsm.com

Reviews make and/or recommend improvements. Ideally these are inputs to a continual service improvement (CSI) programme.

Adapt

Case Management is made adaptive to a changing environment through our existing ITSM improvement processes, where present. Cases should be reviewed for potential improvements for all the Case Management resources, especially the templates/models and the knowledgebase.

Case reviews create a **self-adapting system** so that process stays current with some of the changes in our environment by creating and capturing best workflows for new standard types of response, e.g. provisioning users to a previously unknown system, or resetting a new type of handheld device.

We standardise our process models for known response types. As the world changes, suddenly we get new kinds of exceptions. Case Management deals with the exceptions. The review process captures repeat exceptions and recognises new process models which we standardise and then feed back into the knowledgebase, so that they will be handled as Standard models in future not Cases, thereby adapting to the changing environment.

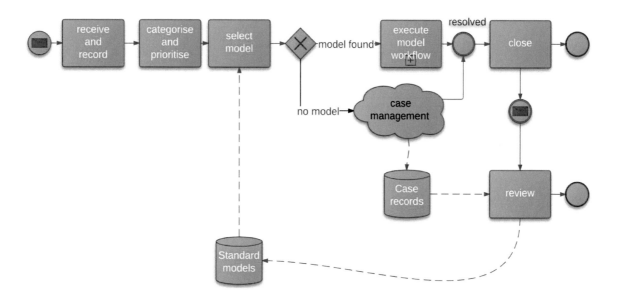

This is far more adaptive than the Standard model on its own, and Standard+Case extends the Case Management approach as well to allow it to formalise Standard responses.

We discussed a request catalogue that covered only 60% of incoming requests and had no mechanism to deal with the other 40%. Standard+Case would deal with them using Case Management, then over time S+C would capture the new request types through review and encapsulate them as Standard models.

Chapter

8

Things

We have discussed People and Practices. The third of the three aspects of introducing Standard+Case is Things. Recall most sources talk about "People Process Technology" but "Process" and "Technology" are restrictive words. We want to look at Things: all objects and artefacts in the environment, from technology to documentation.

Policy

There is a school of thought that the most important "Thing" for enabling Case Management is improved access to data, and its visualisation. This thinking stems from IT's fixation with technical solutions to non-technical requirements. Knowledge management is essential but the primary requirement for enabling Case is to empower the case workers, and to do that the essential Thing is clear policy. Contrary to a commonly-held vendor opinion, one single holistic view of customer data and/or business applications doesn't empower staff at all – it is mildly useful at best. Good management communication via policy trumps fancy information tools every time.

Policy should specify:

- the broad and fundamental principles that govern responding

- strategy: why we do what we do

- the overall business goals of the response practices

- the conditions under which Case Management may be used; in other words, what defines the situation for a Case response

- the conditions under which using Case Management is not appropriate or acceptable

- who is entitled to be a case worker: what certifications and approvals are required to do Case Management

- what external and internal controls must be complied with: regulations, standards, frameworks

- what actions a case worker can and cannot perform

- what resources a case worker is entitled to request and use, and how much. This includes budgetary limits

- what inputs and outputs are mandatory for various categories of response

- what the expectations are for behaviour and outcomes

- other business guidelines, rules and bounds

There is no necessity for a separate policy document to govern Case Management. The Case policy should form part of broader policy governing service support.

Strategy

Case workers need insight into the planning and decision making of the organisation. They need enough transparency to know the intent of their goals; to understand why they need to do what they do, why the rules and bounds are what they are, and what the customers need to get. (See "Transparency").

Sharing this will be challenging for many organisations. This is linked to the broader organisational changes needed for the knowledge economy – the move from hierarchal to collaborative models, moving from seeing the organisation as an organism to seeing it as a community. These are much broader transformations than can be addressed in this book.

Architecture

Architecture is almost as important as policy to a case manager, to guide them in what they are doing.

Enterprise Architecture (EA) describes the activities and components of the organisation, now and into the future. It describes the internal and external relationships and dependencies of those components. It defines the patterns for how it all fits together, the standards and rules for how components connect. In other words is the design of all the moving parts of an enterprise.

IT Architecture is the information subset of EA.

If case workers are fixing, changing or replacing those components of the organisation (people, practices, processes, software, infrastructure, plant, facilities, tools, data, suppliers …) then the architectural standards and templates are obviously an essential resource to understand how things are supposed to work and why.

The architecture should describe and interconnect:

- entities and their relationships

- data model (or models: organisations don't always take on the enormous task of a unified data model any more)

- strategy maps

- value streams (or value networks)

- practices (policy, plans, roles, teams, responsibilities, tools, templates, processes, techniques, procedures, work instructions ….)

- capability maps

- organisational structure

Knowledge

Davenport[1] says "knowledge workers can either find knowledge, create it, package it, distribute it, or apply it." In response work, we are mostly applying it.

The goal of knowledge is to complement (not replace) the human mind.

Repository

Don't overestimate the value of knowledge repositories. Without a high investment, including dedicated custodial and educational resources, the author's experience of such repositories is that they last a maximum of two years before a new one is proposed, and often the knowledge is obsolete before they are rolled out. Wikis are especially prone to degenerating into low quality sources of knowledge, and if they don't it is due to one or two passionate custodians.

Nevertheless, good data and meta-data repositories do help improve knowledge distribution with adequate investment and on-going commitment. Often a simple search tool makes a significant difference without reorganising information.[2]

Templates

Think of Case Management templates as non-standard models for executing. They are less formal or complete. Over time we will refine the templates, capturing more knowledge of what works, until some of them will evolve into Standard models, and those models will then be handled by Standard process. Others will never get to be standardised but they still develop over time, improving our capability.

You can store templates in a specialised Case Management tool, or you can store them as text documents. Case workers can interact with them through an active tool, or can read them. The technology should be appropriate to the needs of the organisation (see Software Tools).

Templates should describe:

- business objectives and customer outcomes

---

[1] T. Davenport, *Thinking for a Living*. See bibliography.

[2] Sadly, Google Desktop has been discontinued. Other similar tools can be found here
http://en.wikipedia.org/wiki/List_of_search_engines#Desktop_search_engines

- goals (there may be a range of potential goals depending on the circumstances, some may be mandatory)

- metrics for success

- roles and accountabilities

- capabilities required to succeed

- tasks (perhaps as a checklist)

- architectural information: the inter-relationships and dependencies between business entities, goals, metrics, capabilities, tasks etc.

- workflows that have worked in the past

- required or suggested inputs (checklist, links, sources), including resources, standards, knowledge, and case studies

- required or suggested outputs (checklist, links, samples, document templates), including reporting

Checklists

One simple yet important template mechanism produces proven results in consistency and quality when adopted: checklists. The use of checklists during procedures will reduce error levels and improve performance.

The classic example of checklist use is the book of checklists that all aircraft pilots use to help them deal with a wide range of foreseeable situations.

Case Management checklists do not dictate sequence, just completeness. There will be checklists for required inputs, tasks, and/or outputs.

For some free service management checklists, see the author's site http://www.basicsm.com

These are also known by ACM[1] as an Activity List, which can be presented in Gantt chart format with time bars.

Checklists play an essential part in making sure we know what tasks to do at various points: what actions must, should, or could happen before the case is over; and what artefacts must, should or could be inputs or outputs of the case. This is called the MoSCoW technique: the case worker will consider a checklist and classify the items as "Must Should Could or Won't" be done.

Here are some basic principles to bear in mind when defining checklists. Many of these ideas come from the excellent book *The Checklist Manifesto*[2], which everyone should read.

---

[1] *Mastering the Unpredictable*. See Bibliography.

[2] *The Checklist Manifesto*, Atul Gawande, Metropolitan Books 2009, ISBN 978-0805091748

A checklist is not a teaching tool. It assumes expertise: it talks the user's language and assumes they know what it is talking about (though supplementary explanations are OK if necessary). The checklist is there to prevent errors of omission not errors of ignorance.

A checklist is used during a single procedure, or at a point in time in a procedure (or set of procedures). Don't write a checklist for a wide subject area ("Change checklist").

Checklists may or may not have a defined order or sequence.

There are a few fundamental types of checklist:

- A checklist used during a single procedure is called a READ-DO checklist: read out an item, do it, check it off. This usually has an explicit or implied sequence.

- A checklist used at a point in time or "pause point" in a procedure is a DO-CONFIRM checklist: do what you need to do, then pause to confirm them all on the checklist.

- A CHECK-CONFIRM checklist, used in assessment and audit to ensure all accountabilities, capabilities, controls and activities are in place.

State which type your checklist is.

State what the objective of the checklist is.

Keep the checklist simple. Rules of thumb: no more than ten items, or no more than one minute to perform the check.

IT people tend to crave completeness: don't try to put everything in. The Checklist of Checklists[1] says the items should be:

- a critical step and in great danger of being missed

- not adequately checked by other mechanisms

- actionable, with a specific response required for each item

- designed to be read aloud as a verbal check

- one that can be affected by the use of a checklist

---

[1] *A Checklist of Checklists*, Atul Gawande
http://www.projectcheck.org/uploads/1/0/9/0/1090835/checklist_for_checklists_group_draft_5.pdf

Procedures

Although there is no formal process that a case worker is required to follow for resolution of a case, there will be procedures (or "sub-processes") that will be commonly executed. There is clearly benefit in formalising these using traditional BPM, measuring and improving them, and even automating some of them.

They would then be made available to the case workers as resources they can use. For example:

- procuring supplies

- engaging another agency or team

- getting approvals or decisions

- (re-)planning how to deal with the state

- existing support procedures

Model and Notation

The Open Management Group (OMG, not the usual meaning of the acronym) is developing the Case Management Model and Notation (CMMN). The notation will allow the case worker to plan process elements, resources, and file structure for a case. For example a case is an entity, containing:

- a case file

- a case life cycle

- a planning pallet

- a set of case roles

- taxonomies of plan-able elements

This convention for describing case management "process" is still under revision and voting within the OMG at the time of writing (early 2013).

There is a school of thought that Business Process Modelling Notation, BPMN, could be extended to support case management but the OMG (who also own BPMN) has chosen to adopt a distinct notation that is not about predefined sequences of tasks.

Software Tools

Case is about the approach people use, not the tools. Don't seek a technical fix to a non-technical requirement. Current tools will often be good enough.

> …Case Management, rather than being a new technology, is actually just a new way of thinking about how the technology we use integrates with the services we provide.[1]

A perfect software tool is not an essential condition for successful Case Management. One shouldn't decline to adopt a better way because the current tool doesn't support it. Either:

(a) use the current tool for managing requests and branch to a different tool for the Case Management or

(b) find a way to manage Cases in the existing tool even if it wasn't designed for it and extend the tool where necessary or

(c) look for a new tool with both Case Management and BPM capabilities.

Your incumbent ticketing tool will generally be adequate. The greatest area of concern is that Case requires advanced knowledge management capabilities. ITSM tools have matured greatly in this area in recent years. In addition, many of us have resorted to a separate knowledge management tool where the ticketing tools were not strong enough. (We encounter the same issue when one tries to implement Knowledge Centered Support, for example).

Integration is over-rated. Who cares if the ticketing system doesn't link to the content management system and you have to copy and paste links into tickets? The tools will come soon enough once vendors detect a market. Get the people and practices under way first.

Off-the-shelf systems exist for other sectors such as law, police, medicine and social work, but they are unlikely to be useful to IT or other sectors without extensive adaptation.

Don't seek technical solutions to non-technical challenges.
Case is about behaviour.
Tools assist.

Some Case Management support can be found within existing process workflow tools that take a conventional BPM approach: modelling tasks and "default" templates of workflows that include provision for certain Events, and that can be adapted by the user at execution.

The IT analyst group Forrester sees[2] Case Management as a hybrid of enterprise content management, BPM, data analytics, and social computing interfaces.

In organisations with advanced requirements for tools to enhance the efficiency and effectiveness of S+C response, there are a wide range of technologies to draw from: transactional ticketing

---

[1] Social Solutions, http://www.socialsolutions.com/blog/advanced-case-management-an-overview/

[2] *Dynamic Case Management – an Old Idea Catches Fire*, C Le Clair and C Moore, Forrester 2009

systems, process modelling and workflow, knowledge sharing, decision automation, expert systems, data mining, analytics, reporting, portals, collaboration tools and so on. An in-depth discussion of the support of knowledge work with tools is outside the scope of this book.

Adaptive Case Management is another tools-centric approach to implementing case management. Swenson[1] describes it as a Lean approach:

> Using "design for people, build for constant change" principles is a more Lean approach than structured, predictable, mass-production approaches automated with BPM suites

This is ironic given Lean's emphasis on standardisation, repeatability and efficiency. It is true that ACM is an extremely adaptable approach to automating case management (see "Review and Improve"). Tools based on ACM principles bear close consideration, as tools that are designed based on the principles of Case Management rather than extending conventional Standard process tools.

Human Interaction Management tools manage the six different kinds of objects defined by HIM: Roles, Users, Interactions, Entities, States, and Activities[2]. HIM tools are used to manage collaboration, either collaboration specific to a case, or ad-hoc. They need to connect or integrate in some way with the tools used to drive BPM and Case, to link the collaboration to the activities.

Criteria for a S+C tool

The ideal S+C tool would provide these capabilities for the case worker (not administrator or programmer) to do dynamically during the resolve step of the ticket:

- A status of "managing case" within requests, incidents, problems, changes (and perhaps other ticket types like work assignments, events etc.)

- Define goals.

- Define current case state, possible actions, resources.

- Dynamically create and change the workflow.

- Set calendar deadlines and reminders against ticket and tasks.

- Assign ticket and tasks to owners. Link and manage other participants.

- Embed business rules (hard) and guidelines (soft) in functionality (but see notes below about Automation)

- Enable collaboration and decision-making.

- Capture and store all communications.

- Create an audit trail of the ticket history including communications.

---

[1] *Mastering the Unpredictable.* See Bibliography.

[2] *The Greatest Innovation Since BPM*, P Fingar, BPTrends March 2007 http://www.bptrends.com

- Attach rich content, or link the ticket to content management system objects. Content will include documents, scanned documents, images, audio, video, chat, web content, emails and so on.

- Visualisation and navigation of the rich content.

- Sharing and controlled distribution of content.

- Integral knowledge management or link the ticket to objects in a knowledge management system.

- Provide access to all the business applications that case workers will need.

- KCS-compliant capabilities to rank and improve knowledge[1]

  - integration with external (web) knowledge

  - intelligent search

  - formatting of ticket information

  - hyperlinking in knowledgebase and ticket text

  - capture ticket information into knowledge articles

  - many-to-many linking between tickets and knowledge

  - advanced metadata on knowledge articles

  - publishing knowledge content to the web

  - flag knowledge content as needing work; provide feedback; ratings

  - analysis of knowledge usage

  - report on individuals' knowledge usage and contribution

  - quality measurement and control

- Apply a template(s) when we change to Case status not when the ticket is created.

- Templates to set goals, create workflow or a list of tasks, attach rich content.

- Create a digitally signed archive package on close.

- If you adopt a longitudinal approach, then the tool will need to manage cases and sub-cases, and provide CRM capabilities to manage the long-term relationship with a customer and their users.

You may not find tools that meet all or even most of those requirements. Don't over-invest in trying to create one until the Case Management practice is mature enough that tool requirements have become clear. Tools are used to increase efficiency and effectiveness of the procedures: to make them faster and to reduce errors – you need to find the bottlenecks and sources of error first.

---

[1] For more information see
http://www.serviceinnovation.org/included/docs/cert/verified_v5_selfassess_worksheets.xls

Maturity of tools

There is a maturity model for the use of software to support Case Management, called C3M[1] because it looks at three aspects of case at each maturity level: characterisations, benefits, and risks.

Remember this model is about using IT tools in the Case approach (in sectors such as social work or health... or IT), not about using Case approach in an IT context. According to the C3M authors, "to the best of our knowledge, no maturity models for case management exist in literature".

The C3M maturity levels are similar to the generic CMM levels. They are:

Individualistic	Each case worker organises their own information using generic desktop and office tools
Supported	Specialised case handling software organises information; controls access; and provide some simple templates and automation
Managed	Cases are managed and planned as portfolios (groups of cases), and their information aggregated.
Standardised	Business rules and guidelines are embedded in software, especially for assessments. The software provides visualisation of the case.
Transformative	Analytical and matching capabilities look for similarities and identify best practices to improve case management.

Automation

Hopefully automation won't come up too often in the context of Case Management. A classic area for over-investment in the IT sector is in automation of IT procedures. Because IT is so successful at automating larger-scale procedures within the rest of the business, we think such automation will scale down to internal IT functions. This is often a fallacy: the ROI of automation is scale-sensitive.

You should only automate that which is

- **repeatable** and strictly, clearly defined. This closely corresponds to our S+C definition of Standard.

- **frequent** (or very expensive). It costs a lot to automate. There need to be enough transactions to provide a return on investment (ROI).

---

[1] *Capabilities and Levels of Maturity in IT-based Case Management*, J Koehler, J Hofstetter, R Woodtly, Proc. 10th Int. Conference on Business Process Management (BPM-2012), Springer, LNCS

An Impact-oriented Maturity Model for IT-based Case Management, J. Koehler, R. Woodtly, J. Hofstetter http://user.enterpriselab.ch/~takoehle/publications/bpm/C3MWithRiskMap.pdf

- **stable**. It costs a lot to change automation, just like it costs a lot to change any production software-based system. If the rules or procedure are always changing then people flex and change faster and more cheaply than automation software can.

In the IT sector, not many procedures fit all three of those criteria. Case Management is particularly ill-suited to automation: it is unpredictable, variable and relatively infrequent.

Testing the software - whether it be to do IT automation or anything else - far exceeds the cost of coding and usually exceeds the cost of planning and design. This is frequently overlooked by IT staff automating IT systems, who think that banging out another rule or script or template or workflow is a few hours' work.

If the business is automating a core process, then the system is usually properly designed, built, and tested. Our IT tools should be treated as production systems just like the business systems we steward. Our IT tools need to be subject to the same justification, planning, specification, design, testing and release as any other system.

When IT automation is considered properly and its cost calculated as total cost of ownership (TCO) over time, it is less often a good idea.

> Knowledge work is not routine... When it comes to work automation, any advantage gained from similarities is overwhelmed by the additional costs of having to accommodate the differences[1]

Case Management will not usually be a good fit for automated systems.

---

[1] *Mastering the Unpredictable*. See Bibliography.

A Standard+Case Tale[1]

A red line of text appears on Danny's screen. The monitor on the internal chat system has picked up a staff member complaining of being unable to access the client management system, ERNIE. Danny grins: the "#fail" keyword always gets the social monitor's attention. Danny opens an Incident ticket. Another day on the Service Desk.

He looks her up on the HR system to find her location. Danny is a one-star Service Desk Analyst, certified to run basic network diagnostics. It was a 2 hour CBT and a simple 10 minute online exam. Danny tries to do one new certification every week: part of his bonus is based on the number of certifications he accumulates.

So he runs the diagnostics but can't find any problems at her location. If it was affecting everyone the phones would be running hot and there'd be something on the Service Desk console by now.

Perhaps it is PBCAK (problem between chair and keyboard). He calls her. A lucky day, she actually answers. No "nilm" required on the ticket history ("not in, left message").

"Hello Inge, this is Danny from the Service Desk. I saw your comment on Chatter. Having problems with ERNIE?"

It turns out Inge knows exactly what she is doing, but her location is out of date on the HR system. Danny always enjoys things like that: it guarantees that automation isn't going to do him out of a job any time soon. Danny likes being a Service Desk Analyst - it is the most rewarding job he has had. And here at BigMed he knows his pay will be pretty good within a few years as he builds seniority through further certifications, accreditations, performance, and experience.

Danny runs a quick check for the correct location while she waits, and finds nothing. He takes remote control of her desktop (another certification he has – it included a whole lot of privacy policy questions along with the technical ones). He finds a configuration issue on her desktop client.

He categorises the Incident ticket accordingly. There is no automated workflow in the ticketing tool for that category of Incident, but there is a solution in the knowledgebase with a scripted series of steps to fix the configuration properly, and a checklist of everything that should be in place

---

[1] Clearly inspired by *The Phoenix Project*, G. Kim, K. Behr, G. Spafford, IT Revolution Press 2013, ISBN 978-0988262591, an excellent parable on the benefits of DevOps.

when finished. Danny clicks the "thumbs down" on the script – it is a bit confusing. He dashes off a quick comment. The solution's use-count increments by one: Danny can see it gets quite a lot of use. Negative feedback and high use: Danny knows the solution will bubble up to the top of the QA queue, and he or someone else on the team will look into it soon. There are good status points to be earned for knowledge improvement work, and the whole team have learned to treasure their knowledgebase as the thing that most contributes to making their job easier. He chuckles to himself: he remembers when he learned the lesson. He came in one day with a monster hangover. He'd never have made it through the day without the knowledgebase.

Danny has also learned to always follow the script. The Service Delivery Coordinator and the Service Desk team leader both do random QA audits of closed tickets. Staff have been busted down the seniority tables for not following a standardised procedure when one exists. Besides, the scripts and checklists and automated workflows had saved his butt uncounted times when he nearly forgot something.

Access restored. Inge is happy and agrees the ticket can be closed. That's one more on his First Call Resolution stats.

Danny is about to hang up when Inge, obviously inspired by Danny's helpfulness, asks "What do I do about a dead client?" It turns out someone came in for an appointment but ERNIE showed them as deceased. Inge has all the details on paper but is still trying to work out how to process the appointment for a cadaver.

Danny opens a new Incident ticket and captures as much detail as he can from Inge while he has her on the phone, but regretfully tells her the Service Desk will have to get back to her. That's one less on his FCR stats. Never mind, plenty more where that came from.

Danny knows dead people don't arrive for appointments so he sets the Incident situation code to "unknown".

He knows he is out of his depth – this isn't going to be a First Level Resolution for him either. A quick glance at the case workers' Kanban board shows that Lee is only handling two cases at the moment. Danny changes the Incident status to "case", assigns it to the Case queue and calls Lee. She is accredited by the vendor of ERNIE as a Level 2 technician – she can handle it.

After Lee gets off the phone from Danny, she picks up the Incident off the queue, assigns it to herself, and adds the third case to her Kanban column. That's her full up: no more than three cases in progress at a time. Next year she'll have enough seniority to handle four cases at a time, with a consequent pay increment.

Lee logs on to ERNIE. The client is indeed dead, according to ERNIE. Lee considers the state of the Case:

> Situation: wrongly dead client. There is no administrative function to change the status once a patient is dead.

> Goal: change their status code to "active".

Action: Lee will need the DBA to make a direct change to the client's database record. Policy says this has to be done as a Change, but there have been enough other issues with ERNIE data requiring direct DBA intervention that such changes have been designated as a Standard Change (ERNIE is a bit flaky). Lee opens a Standard Change ticket. Because it is Standard Change it is pre-approved so she assigns it directly to the DBA group queue.

You don't get to be a case worker without developing some instincts. While she waits for the DBAs to action the change, Lee opens the Audit Log on ERNIE and searches to see what idiot marked the patient as dead. No idiot. There is no audit log of a status change on that patient.

Next, Lee goes to the Change ticket database and searches for Standard Changes to ERNIE data for the "deceased" status code. There are seven others this year. Warren – her least favourite case worker - has requested four of them. She calls Warren.

"Warren, it's Lee here"

"Hello Lee". Warren doesn't sound enthused to hear from Lee.

"Did you know you have requested four patients be raised from the dead in ERNIE so far this year?"

"Yes there have been a couple of those. Someone is killing our clients."

"It's not funny Warren. Did you check who marked them deceased? I'll save you the trouble. No-one did: there's no audit record. Did it occur to you there might be a Problem here?"

"No it didn't Lee. I had more important things to worry about. We play God, we get them marked alive again. Problem solved ok?"

"No the Problem isn't solved! Only the incident is. There's a Problem out there: something is falsely setting that code to 'deceased'."

"Go get 'em Lee, you're the ace detective. Let me know how it works out."

Lee fumes as she hangs up. She opens a Problem ticket linked to the Incident, and assigns it to herself. As the most highly accredited staff member for ERNIE, Lee deals with Problems on ERNIE when she isn't fully occupied on Cases.

Lee schedules an online conference with Simon from 3Thimbles Tech, the vendor of ERNIE, and two BigMed staff: Ann, the applications developer who works on ERNIE integration, and Russell the IT security analyst (if audit records are missing he needs to be involved).

The conference battles with all the usual issues of people talking over each other, fractured video, and slow graphics on the shared online whiteboard. Lee pines for the days when people actually got together in a room, but at least the conference happened quickly.

The team apply all their regular tools: a situational analysis, a barrier analysis, a brainstorm, and a root cause analysis.

They soon focus on two essential clues

- the missing audit record
- all the accidentally-deceased clients were transferred from two particular external clinics

This unravels the cause. The two clinics are the only external agencies who use the BERC4 patient management system. Patient records are transferred into BigMed's ERNIE through a complex system of scripted batch feeds called GLUE. Updates from the external agencies are also applied via GLUE. GLUE doesn't write ERNIE audit records; it has its own basic log. It is a known issue that has caused heated debate, but GLUE was written quickly when the ERNIE implementation project ran short of funds and the properly designed integration system using expensive 3Thimbles services was cut.

Ann needs an hour to trawl the GLUE log, so the conference call disbands. Russell from security clearly thinks it was a waste of his time (but policy said he had to be there), and Simon the vendor manages to impart a strong "I told you so" message without actually saying anything. But Lee is unfazed: she has her result. She knows it already, in her gut.

While she waits, Lee checks the Standard Change to resurrect the original client. Nobody has picked it up from the DBAs' queue so she rings the DBA team leader and applies a little pressure.

Lee's gut was right. Ann comes back looking shame-faced. She physically turns up at Lee's desk, so Lee can see the embarrassment as Ann explains that the table which maps BERC4 status codes to ERNIE status codes has an error. When BERC4 updates their status to "in remission", GLUE maps that to an ERNIE code of "deceased". Ann has tested it in the User Acceptance environment and will ask one of the external clinics to run a transaction against a test patient in Production. The mapping table has been fixed; there will be no more wrongly deceased patients.

The testing of GLUE was another project shortcut.

Lee consoles Ann but also adds "Sorry Ann but I think this Problem is sure to be flagged for review because of the client impact. They may put this on the weekly Intelligence Report". Ann sighs and goes back to nursing GLUE along.

Lee updates the Problem record and puts it into a waiting status until Ann completes the production test. Lee has her own informal checklist of things to go over after an application problem is found. She runs through it now, and reminds herself she must publish it to the team knowledgebase. It would be useful for them, and besides she needs to get her five new solutions published before month end.

An alert pops up to tell her the Standard Change has been closed. Lee logs on to ERNIE and sure enough the client lives again.

Lee updates the Incident ticket with the actions taken and the result, then changes the ticket status from "Case" to "Resolved". She smiles: she is chasing the 50-A-Month badge that the case workers covet. It also rewards her with an extra day's leave but it is the badge she really wants, to show to Warren. He's never had one; it will be her third.

She runs through the case resolution checklist to ensure she has done and written everything required. Problem ticket: check. History detail updated: check. Cost and effort estimate recorded: check. Medical impact and risk flagged: check. Nothing else applies to this one.

Lee transfers the Incident back to Danny, the Incident owner. When Danny sees it come up on his queue he calls Inge. No need to tell her all the details of the screw-up, but he thanks her for bringing it to their attention and assures her it shouldn't happen again as the underlying Problem has been resolved. Inge agrees to close the Incident.

Danny is about to hang up and start the incident closure checklist when Inge says "Hey, while you are on the line, I've got another question…"

Inge has a query about her last payslip, something about payment for a public holiday. Danny has no payroll support certifications, so he puts Inge on hold, checks the Service Desk console, sees that George is off the phone and has the required certification, and transfers the call to George. While George answers, Danny opens a new Incident ticket and transfers it to George. Danny always does it that way: you are recognised for your throughput of tickets. Besides, it does George a small favour too.

Now Danny wraps up the original ticket. He pulls up the incident closure checklist and checks them all off:

- ☑ Confirm that the Incident is resolved
- ☑ Confirm that recovery is complete: the service has been restored to the user
- ☑ User agrees the incident can be closed
- ☑ Check that Incident is in the right category and correct if necessary
- ☑ Check that Incident is associated with the correct asset(s)
- ☑ Ensure that the Incident history is a complete record
- ☑ Ensure that Incident documentation is complete
- ☑ Determine whether the information in the Incident record should be part of the knowledgebase, and take the necessary action to copy it there
- ☑ If it is likely that the incident could recur, check whether there is an existing Problem record, or create one
- ☑ Link the Incident to any related Master-Incident, Problem or Change records
- ☑ Close the Incident

So he does.

Adopting Standard+Case

Remember your organisation is almost certainly using a Case approach already: we seek to formalise what is done.

S+C does not propose any new practice. It is an extension to existing ITSM practices. Service Case Management impacts Service Desk, Level 1, Level 2, Level 3, Service Delivery, and Technical Operations. It potentially modifies the way we do Request, Incident, Problem, Change, Supplier, and Service Level Managements.

Implement Case Management once. Set up ownership, policy, roles, procedures, resources, and tools once for Case Management, to be used as a common discipline in all contexts within your organisation, whatever function/team and process/procedure it is used in.

Here is a suggested simple step-by-step approach to adopting Standard+Case:

1) If what you do now is all Case, then keep doing what you do now. You are no worse off.

2) Get the Review activity working: review a selection of Cases.

3) Start improving by standardising. Review will tell you which are the common easy responses to standardise: e.g. password reset, Active Directory privileges, new phone, desktop move etc... Every response you standardise is one more that you can measure and control.

4) A new Standard response may well point to a new problem in the system. Problem management should review all newly-identified Standard response types before you put work into creating a model response.

5) Let people know they are being monitored. Report failures to use an existing Standard Model. Over time put the squeeze on. E.g. failure to use a Standard category means you get put on dealing with instances of that category until you learn to recognise it.

6) Once the Standard volume grows big enough, being a case worker becomes a privilege.

7) Later look at how you measure and improve the hopefully-shrinking pool of Case responses. Understand demand: what kind of cases do we get, what are the sources, what value does resolution represent to the customers, and what patterns are there. From that information, we can prioritise and contextualise our improvement work.

Business case

No pun intended.

The business case for making the initial effort to adopt the Standard+Case approach and to implement Case Management needs to be constructed like any business case: by determining the organisational value of the outcomes in terms of extra revenue, reduced costs, reduced risk, and/or delivery of compliance; and then ensuring they exceed the cost and impact of doing it.

Standard+Case offers the following tangible benefits:

- better utilisation of staff resources through greater throughput of responses because of more effective and efficient resolution of unknown and unfamiliar situations

- reduced user down-time and time spent waiting on responses

- fewer errors in complex and complicated situations.

Standard+Case offers the following less tangible benefits:

- greater flexibility in responding to user needs

- higher customer and user satisfaction

- improved staff morale

- better metrics: greater predictability of Standard responses and more meaningful monitoring of Case responses

The costs of adopting Standard+Case will hopefully not be too large, since we are formalising what already exists. Costs may include:

- establishing a Case Management practice (roles, training, resources, and tools)

- changes to categorisation, service level targets, and reporting

- changes to response procedures, especially transfer and review

- changes to service improvement practice

- creating a mechanism and process for certification and accreditation of staff

- allowing slack capacity to deal with unpredictability

You may have good metrics for what proportion of responses are Standard and how many are Case, but if not, start at 50% of each until you have better information.

Customers

As we discussed under "Service levels" above, we want to change the way we measure and set targets for service levels (SLTs) for those responses that turn out to be cases, i.e. non-standard. This may be a difficult sell to some customers, who will see it as a way of removing some responses from the existing service level commitments, i.e. a cop-out.

We need to convince the customer that a Service Level Agreement that separates our SLTs into different Standard and Case categories is in fact a better reflection of reality, allows tighter commitments, and provides more accurate measurement.

A time-based SLT for unfamiliar situations is delusional. The world simply does not work like that: every case is unpredictable. By separating out the familiar form the unfamiliar, we actually improve our ability to predict and deliver on Standard situations: we can give the customer a _tighter_ time-based SLT for Standard responses because we are removing a large cause of variability in existing measurements which mix up the two.

Any relationship works on trust and verification. For case responses, the SLA should commit to targets for the actions and resources we will commit to providing for different priority levels of Case; and it should commit to the verification mechanisms we provide for the customer to review our performance in case management. It can also commit to other metrics that work for cases (see "Measurement"). If we promised the customer anything else than this, we would be feeding the delusion.

Owner

Case Management should have an owner, who is responsible for the central administration of resources and tools to support case wherever it is performed in the organisation, to

- provide support and resources for each of the practice owners

- provide training and certification

- ensure consistency in Case Management across practices that use it

- acquire, provide, and support any specialised Case Management tools

Note: this is an owner for the whole Case Management discipline, not to be confused with the fact that each case has a designated owner of that case. Think of it as a Case Management Office, analogous to a Project Management Office (PMO).

This is a role not a job description: like all ITSM roles, the Case Owner role is assigned to someone as part of a broader job function, such as Service Delivery Manager, Architect, Technical Manager, or Operations Support. It is "a hat you wear".

The Standard+Case journey

Most descriptions of Service Management and Case Management are either idealised (what the perfect system looks like), or comprehensive (everything you could possibly consider), or both.

The world doesn't work like that: we don't build everything at once and we don't build perfectly first time. Don't try to do it all at once: don't try to do all areas and don't try to do all of one area.

Start

Start with the bits you need the most – and where the quick wins are - and do as much as you need to get what you need.

How to decide what you need? Don't introduce Standard+Case thinking because it seems like a good idea. Do it because there is some business improvement or result required – "a gain or a pain" - and Standard+Case just happens to be the best way to get there: e.g. lower cost customer support, fewer disastrous rollouts, happier customers, better data on products, introducing a more complex service...

So there is no substitute for looking at your own situation to decide what to work on.

One strategy is to properly review the situation. Where are you at now? Where do you need to be and by when? What is the gap? This results in a clearer big picture of where you need to improve. Sometimes it helps to get an objective external view from experts; other times they "borrow your watch to tell you the time".

Another strategy is to simply list the "pains" or risks and to prioritise them, then have at them one by one. This is more of an incremental approach. The risk is that you might deal with the urgent rather than the important.

Either way, start with a business objective; then plan and design the solution to get it; and only then adopt the bits of service management needed in that solution.

Transform

You don't "do" or implement" or "create" Case Management, even though we use phrases like these all the time. You transform or improve it. Case Management is there in your organisation already. Perhaps it is done badly or so little it is undetectable, but it is there. Have a mindset of building on what is already there, of improving, of increasing capability.

Even though this book describes many aspects of Standard+Case, that doesn't mean you take all of this book and adopt it right away (though it is so basic that we hope you will do most of it pretty soon).

Plan an approach to the transformation. Include steps to address people, practices and things, discussed in detail in the rest of this book. If the planned cost and effort is not spread near to equally across each of those three aspects that would be a cause for concern.

Continue

Even though you don't have to improve for ever, don't stop once you have done what you set out to do, for three reasons:

1)   Anything left alone will run down. You need to keep it alive, keep it working.

2)   The world changes, requirements shift. You need to be continually adjusting.

3)   Most organisations want to continue to improve, to keep getting better

That is why we called it a journey – you are never done. Service Management transformation is not a project with an end-date. Assign it to an owner, make them accountable. It is continual not necessarily continuous: you don't have to work on it every day but you do need to keep coming back to it. Get into a continual cycle of: Check your current state; Plan where you want to be and how to get there; Act to make it happen. [1]

Too many change programmes lose momentum because management move on or lose interest. This has facetiously been described as Plan-Do-Stop. This is why you need an on-going formal programme of work to provide continuity and permanence.

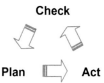

Introducing improvements

Culture

Services are delivered by people for people to people. There is no more important factor in service success than people: their culture (behaviours and beliefs), their development, their motivation, and your communication. All change to services (new ones, improvements) is change to people: changing their attitudes, their behaviours, their daily practices and habits.

What is more, successful service providers need staff with a healthy service culture. Unlike products, services touch users directly. In order to deliver a service your staff must interact with the users.

It is hard to change the culture of your organisation: the beliefs and habits, "the way things are done around here". The surface effect of that culture – the "climate" – is easier to change: the practices and habits of people. Over time repeated behaviour and changed attitudes sink in to change the culture. So one way to gradually shift culture is to change the rules and procedures. If you change what people do, you will change how they feel about it and eventually what they believe.

---

1   The most common version of this cycle is known as the Deming Cycle of Plan-Do-Check-Act, but we think Check-Plan-Act makes a more logical cycle. We first saw it in *Understanding Your Organisation as a System*, Vanguard Consulting, 2001, http://www.systemsthinking.co.uk/5-1.asp

As well as influencing behaviour, you can also directly influence deeper attitudes, and even the underlying beliefs, through persuasion, education and example. It takes more time and effort but it yields more results.

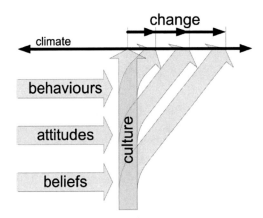

Spend a serious chunk of the money allocated for improving service on improving your people: communicate, involve, motivate, consult (pick their brains), communicate, train, incent, communicate, monitor and coach.

Technology changes at blinding speed these days but people and practices don't. Real organisational improvement must be incremental and at a human pace. Pushing change too fast breaks culture.

An important concept is "line of sight": no matter how deep they are in the "back office" functions of an organisation, try to give people line of sight to the customer. That is, keep reminding them of how they affect the customer's result and the user's experience. Develop empathy for the consumer and understanding of the user's needs. The best way to do this is to expose staff to users: meet and talk.

As well as bottom-up "grass roots" influences, we can also change culture from the top down, via the leadership: the figurehead leader, the executive team, the managers. They have a large influence on the climate or personality of the organisation and they can shift culture in only a few years by what they say and even more so by what they are seen to do. Selecting and directing them are the governors who therefore also have an influence.

Sometimes a group within the organisation who do not formally have a lot of power can still be influencing culture. One example is the corrosive influence of unhappy people: the most negative are also usually the most vocal. Another example is the remains of an absorbed organisation who cling on to their old culture inside the larger one (this can be good or bad but usually bad – you want everyone on the same page).

Great people make shaky practices work well, and good practices deal with poor technology. But it doesn't work in reverse: the best practices in the world will achieve little without getting the people right first; and without good people and good practices, any new technology is a waste of money. Good culture is dependent on good management. Good culture cannot thrive in an organisation with poor management. This book is not about transforming management. There are many books on that topic[1].

Make change happen[2]

Change is driven from a high level. It needs the commitment of the top executive. Without that it is much more difficult.

Change is an on-going programme, with no end.

Talk change over with those who will be affected by it, and those who will have to do it, and those who will have to pay for the effort.

If you have drummed up enthusiasm, get a small team together. Find one or two champions who will push it along. Set up a steering group of bosses and experts to keep it on track.

Do the vision thing: define what you want to achieve and why, and come up with a concise way to say that. Then get the team doing some hard work selling the idea to everyone who will be affected.

Work out what might get in the way (including people), and how to overcome or remove obstacles.

Make people accountable and measure them. Improvement is hard unless a single person has ownership, and is answerable and empowered.

Find a few quick wins. Do something that shows good early results – nothing convinces sceptics better than results.

Don't invent stuff yourselves where you don't need to: draw from outside. This book lists some important resources: set one or two on your team to become your resident experts on case management and service management theory. Also find external people who have done what you want to do before: talk it over; hire their experience if you need to.

Use early successes to build momentum. Progressively work up to bigger and better things. People accept evolution more readily than revolution.

Don't lose what you achieve. Get it embedded in the way things are done, in people's practices and habits, in the rules and the metrics and the policy of your organisation.

We cannot stress enough that any transformation of service management - or the introduction of new services - which ignores the people aspects will at best yield less than it could have, and at worst it will fail … sometimes spectacularly and sometimes slowly crumbling over time.

---

[1] We highly recommend *First Break All The Rules,* M Buckingham and C Coffman, Simon and Shuster 1999, ISBN 0-684-85286-1.

[2] This section was based on John Kotter's 8-step change model (ref 3)

Changing people

People don't change on their own. They need motivation, development, and communication.

Motivate them in these ways: by getting them involved and consulted; by showing how they benefit from the change; by making them accountable and measuring that accountability; and by incenting them.

Development is not just one training course. Training should be followed up, refreshed, and repeated for new entrants. Training is not enough: practical workshops, on-the-job monitoring, coaching support, local super-users and many other mechanisms all help people learn what they need to make change successful.

Communicate early, communicate often, and be as transparent about decision-making as you can. Tough decisions are more palatable if people understand why. Communication is two-way: consult, solicit feedback (including anonymous), run workshops and town-halls.

Employees will commit to a manager's decision – even one they disagree with – if they believe that the process the manager used to make the decision was **fair**[1]. There are three principles of fair process:

- **Engagement**. People need to feel involved and consulted in the decision-making process. They want to be heard.

- **Explanation**. People must understand why the decision was made the way it was. The decision process should be transparent.

- **Expectation** clarity. Once a decision is made, everyone should be clear on what that now means: what has changed, how things will be assessed differently. The new rules should be communicated.

---

[1] *Fair Process: Managing in the Knowledge Economy*, W. C. Kim and R. Mauborgne, Harvard Business Review 1997

Policy

Review existing policy to find a suitable place for the policy governing Case, e.g. you could include Case policy in an Operations policy or a Support policy. It is usually better to embed Case policy in an existing document that to proliferate more policies. To establish Case policy (or any sort of policy):

- Review existing directives from the governors of the organisation, and existing higher-level policies. What does this Case policy need to align/comply with?

- Work with senior management who will be affected by the activities and outputs of Case Management. What goals should Case have? What rules and bounds need to be put on case workers' activities?

- Determine who is the decision maker(s) about Case policy, and who are the other Subject Matter Experts (SMEs).

- Interview the decision maker and SMEs.

- Capture all known policy (goals/objectives, bounds, rules, guidelines) into a policy document or tool. If there is little or no policy in existence yet, never mind: create an empty or minimal policy. The following mechanism will start filling it.

- Review it with the decision maker and up the chain of command to all necessary approvers.

- Review it and perform walkthroughs of scenarios with case workers to ensure it is useful.

- Once content is settled, promote awareness of the policy and educate the affected users of it.

Establish a mechanism to evolve the Case policy:

- Empower workers to act within the policy (and ONLY within the policy).

- Require workers to refer to the decision-maker SME for anything not covered by policy. The mechanism will probably be the original approval process we are replacing, or very similar.

- Coach the decision maker about the bounds of their own authority and the need to go up the chain of command to the appropriate level for making and approving any decision.

- Whenever the decision maker is asked to decide on policy or to clarify policy, the practice owner (or the SME - they have a vested interest in a quiet life) should capture the result in the policy document (and get the SME to confirm the update), so that next time the answer is in the policy and we don't need to bother the SME again.

- Review usage of policy as part of the Review process for selected cases.

- Audit the workers' output for policy compliance. The experts may want to do this themselves or to delegate it to an auditor.

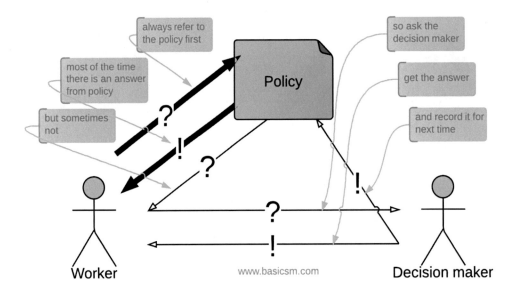

Achieving acceptance of policy is dependent on transparency of decision making: *why* the targets, goals, rules, bounds, and standards are in the policy.

Success of policy relies on the application of Fair Process to its development. (See "Transparency").

Practices

The owners and managers of the existing practices (such as request, incident, change or event) need to extend existing policy, training, staff recognition, measurement, reporting, service levels, resources, tools, and so on, to accommodate Case.

There shouldn't be a great deal of change to existing Request, Incident, Problem, Change processes other than to:

(a) recognise that the Resolve step can branch into a task of Case Management, where the process has a different behaviour (roles, metrics, reporting etc. all change).

(b) remember the importance of Review of selected cases to capture learnings and ensure compliance.

Resources

Make rich resources available to enable case workers to do their best.

Architecture

Enterprise Architecture and IT Architecture define some bounds and rules over what can be built or done, and why. This provides essential context and standards for Case.

So Case Management will need access to architectural information (standards, templates…) as knowledge inputs to cases, and access to architects as people resources for collaboration.

Procedures

There are probably existing procedures documented somewhere in your organisation, which can be absorbed, linked to, copied, or learned from.

Level 2 and 3 Support procedures will involve a lot of case management already. Incidents are escalated to them either because the Standard model requires complex or authorised actions, or because the status is unknown or unfamiliar: there is no standard model. Most of the time it is the latter scenario, which is where Case comes in.

Likewise, the existing Major Incident Management process and procedures – if they exist – will be similar to incident case management. A Major Incident is generally a case.

Problem Management is mostly Case Management: there will be a number of existing resources for root cause analysis etc.

So there will likely be existing procedures and resources that can be captured, formalised and modified to assist Case Management.

Knowledge

Most organisations will have a knowledge management system or systems already. Without one, Case Management will be more difficult.

In implementing Case Management we will impact the knowledge management system by:

- arranging access to knowledge, and to the mechanisms for sharing knowledge between collaborators and clipping knowledge into case records
- expanding the scope of the knowledgebase to meet case workers' needs

Categorisation

It will be a significant change across multiple processes to modify ticketing to indicate when a ticket is being treated as a case.

Your organisation will have multiple parallel taxonomies (ticket attributes or properties) for grouping tickets. You need to work out where "case" fits in your taxonomies. For example, an organisation could:

- add a ticket **status** of "under case management" as an alternative to "resolving"– the easiest option.

- introduce a new **category** of ticket, where we use the term "category" to mean the taxonomy associated with different ways of dealing with the ticket, i.e. the category indicates which Standard model to use. "Case" acts as an "Other" or "Unfamiliar/Unknown" category.

- add a new **type** of ticket called Case alongside Request, Incident, Problem and Change. This is not recommended but it is not ruled out.

Service Providers

Standard+Case sheds new light on outsourcing of response handling, e.g. outsourcing a service desk.

Whether you outsource only the Standard part or Case as well depends on the service provider's skills and expertise.

When outsourcing Standard responses you can use statistics to establish baselines for the supplier's performance; establish "pay per ticket" cost models; and agree normal SLAs based on time to resolve.

But under Case Management you never know in advance which resources, skills and knowledge will be needed.

So traditional outsourcing arrangements are good for Standard responses, whereas a consulting service ("a pool of specialists that I can use under demand when I need them and that you, outsourcer, will rent to many customers to permit scale economies") is a better approach for outsourced Case Management.

You need a higher level of trust to outsource Case to a service provider. It might be a capability you decide to keep in-house.

Support for Standard+Case

See the http://www.basicsm.com/standard-case website for case studies and other resources as they emerge.

There is a private Standard+Case user community on Google+, where we encourage discussion and the sharing of resources (contact the author). I am always happy to talk with those adopting the approach.

Please provide feedback. There may be another edition of this book, if there are sufficient corrections, additions, ideas, and requests for further information.

Contact the author at http://www.basicsm.com/contact.

Standard+Case in the wild

Case Management is in use in ITSM, but not widely. The author has not been able to track down any IT practitioners yet – please contact me.

The Adaptive Case Management community is applying IT tools to the management of cases in many sectors. Case studies (pun probably intended) in the ACM books only include one use of Case Management within an ITSM context: a "Fortune-500 bank in India" using ACM for customer request management.

At the time of going to print, three organisations were trialling the ideas of Standard+Case. Meet the pioneers in the Google+ discussion group and look for case studies on the S+C website.

Learning more about Service Management

This book assumes a basic understanding of Service Management; it is written for Service Management practitioners in general and ITSM practitioners in particular.

If you have struggled with some of the Service Management concepts and terminology, first of all: sorry. Secondly, you can learn more from a number of sources:

- Read this author's book *Basic Service Management*, see www.basicsm.com. I humbly suggest it is the best primer. Or read *The Official Introduction to the ITIL Service Lifecycle V3*, Sharon Taylor, TSO 2007 ISBN 9780113310616.

- There are many more advanced books on Service Management. The definitive refe3rence is *USMBOK*, see the Bibliography.

- Consider doing an ITIL Foundations certification – there are many sources that you can Google online.

Learning more about Case Management

Case Management is a less formalised body of knowledge than Service Management: it is harder to find definitive references that are independent of one particular industry sector.

My recommendation for a first book is *Mastering the Unpredictable*, see the Bibliography. It is a good introduction to Adaptive Case Management (a variant), if a little too technology-centric for this author's tastes.

The Workflow Management Coalition http://www.xpdl.org/nugen/p/adaptive-case-management/public.htm has an excellent online description and resources.

See also the white paper *Case Management*; Kitson, Ravisanskar, Soudamini; Capgemini 2012 http://www.slideshare.net/capgemini/case-management-managing-chaos-unstructured-processes-and-dynamic-bpm

There is a Case Management Body of Knowledge, accessible online by annual subscription. It is focused on health and social welfare cases: cases dealing with people. As such, the usefulness for IT is limited. http://www.cmbodyofknowledge.com/

The Case Manager's Handbook, Fourth Edition is focused on the health industry. It rates highly on Amazon.

The Case Management Societies of America, Australia, and the UK are also focused on health. So is the American Case Management Association.

Case Strategy and Planning

Normally one expects to see "Strategy and Planning" at the start of a book, but this is a practical discussion of the application of Case Management to Service Management. In the real world:

- Many organisations will be too small, fast moving, or informal to ever think about Case strategy.

- Most adoptions of Case Management will start with a trial of the practical use of the approach and only later build out to considerations such as strategy and planning.

- This follows a natural maturity curve: you need to understand Case and see it used and recognise the implications for your organisation before you can do too much meaningful thinking about plans and strategies.

The owner of Case Management as a discipline (the "Case Management Office") will determine a strategy for the introduction and development of Case within the organisation (and perhaps its suppliers).

This strategy must be shaped and informed by the higher-level strategies of the organisation. Case Management needs to understand and work towards the objectives of the department it is used in and the broader organisation it is a part of.

From the strategy, formulate a plan for the introduction and development of Case, covering:

- defining the business case for Case: identify business value and alignment with business objectives

- policy and standards for of Case Management

- developing a Case steering group to provide oversight

- development of resources, methods, and tools

- awareness and promotion of Case amongst potential adopters

- developing a case-worker community and a group of champions

- education programme on Case Management

- certification of case workers

- audit and assessment of cases

- measurement, incentives, and staff KPIs

- improvement of Case Management practices

Please consider Standard+Case

The fundamental principle of Standard+Case is to acknowledge a basic truth: the world is never fully standardised; we will never have a model response for every eventuality. Or even if we did somehow attain that, it wouldn't stay that way for long as the world changes.

So one objective of Standard+Case is to standardise as much as possible, and to move future work from Case to Standard by recognising patterns and creating new Standard models.

But the other objective is to treat the non-standard world as normal, to be managed, reported and improved with the same level of rigour as we do with the standardised part.

Standard+Case introduces Case Management to our thinking for the same reason that we introduced Service Management: to bring in defined practices, mature management, relevant reporting, and structured improvement, so that we can be more effective and efficient at responding to the situations the world presents to us.

Don't leave non-standardised situations to the best efforts of individuals. Don't manage and report them by trying to treat them the same way as standard responses. Don't leave them out of your improvement programme. And don't constrain your staff to doing everything by the book when the world is more complicated than that and your experts can be more creative. Please consider Standard+Case as a better way to think of your service responses.

Appendices

Taxonomy

Image © canstockphoto.com

If you seek to break a rock, many types of stone have a crystal structure which creates fracture planes: hit the rock in the right place and it drops into two; hit it in the wrong direction and it just chips.

When you attempt to categorise stuff into two or more types, if division comes easily and is clear to everyone then you have found a categorisation which reveals something about the underlying nature of the information. If it is hard to divide cleanly, and the results are messy and debatable, then you are trying to force an unnatural taxonomy onto the data.

Image © canstockphoto.com

The author believes ITIL's Incident vs. Request is not a useful categorisation of service responses. I argued this long ago on the IT Skeptic blog[1]. To me an Incident is a sub-type of Request (along with a dozen or so other sub-types). This is not a natural fracture line.

---

[1] www.itskeptic.org

We don't need to debate here whether I'm right or not in that assertion: it is an example of where something doesn't split cleanly and is in fact distracting us from the best way to split service desk response (as an example of responses). Even if you want to maintain the Incident-Request division, Standard+Case is still useful and important to you.

More generally, we shouldn't be focusing on splits by WHAT kind/category of ticket it is. Regardless of the response situation (service desk, change management, tech support, operations...) "WHAT" becomes a many-layered "crumbly" categorisation. The clean split is in HOW we deal with it: Standard or Case.

Looking more closely at that WHAT categorisation, this author suggests a Response taxonomy that differs from ITIL Request in several ways:

- Responses are a generic entity type which is further broken down into types of response, which are child objects inheriting properties of the parent.

- Responses cover Request, Incident, Problem, Change, Event.... any "ticket" which requires a human response.

- Incident is one type of Request, not a totally separate kind of ticket.

- ITIL says all requests should have a model (although it also says "some" in places). S+C says only Standard requests have a model.

Standard+Case suggests a new taxonomy for categorising tickets, but it is not displacing the categorisation by ticket type, it is at right angles to it. Standard+Case is talking about a categorisation of how we *deal* with tickets not *classify* them.

Any one of the classes of Response that we use in order to decide WHAT action is required (whether you use the author's classes or ITIL's), can then be categorised into two classes by HOW we are going to deal with it: Standard process or Case management.

The proportion of Standard to Case will vary from practice to practice, from ticket type to ticket type, but the delineation into the two classes of Standard and Case is quite crisp.

For example many Provisioning (Access) requests will be Standard, but occasionally they will be unusual and need to be dealt with as a Case. Conversely perhaps fewer requests for Help will be Standard, and many will need individual attention as a Case. Many Incidents will be Standard but few Problems will.

None of these many categorisations (WHAT or HOW) should be overly visible to the user. We don't need to tell them that "I am going to handle that as an Incident, in fact a Standard Incident". As far as users are concerned they are all Requests or Responses or Tickets or whatever you want to call them. (Occasionally we do need to explain why we are handling this request different to the user's last one because it is a different type).

For those interested, here is a <u>suggested</u> taxonomy for categorizing Responses[1]. This is the author's own taxonomy and differs from others such as ITIL.

1. Operational Change

A change to a service in a controlled environment, e.g. Production

1.1. Normal

A typical change

1.2. Major

A change which is significant, and requires more consideration and/or control

1.3. Urgent

A change which is needed on a shorter-than-normal timeframe

1.4. Emergency

A change which corrects a problem having a significant impact, so that it is to be implemented outside of normal hours and controls.

1.5. Standard

A change which is standardised and pre-approved.

2. Event

In the ITIL sense not the BPM sense: something which happens in a monitored environment

3. Problem

A cause of an Incident or Incidents - past, present or future

4. Request

A user asks for something. Some theory says that a request must be predefined as part of an agreed Service. S+C understands the world does not work that way: users will ask for all sorts of things. Sometimes the resolution is to say we cannot help, but that is still a response.

4.1. Action

I'd like to say "Service" but that is an exhausted word!

4.1.1. Provisioning

User requires access to a service or part of a service, e.g. a security permission, a menu option, a token, a digital certificate, a client install, a desktop device, a phone, etc.

4.1.2. Booking

E.g. scheduled attendance at training, seminar, meeting, reservation of a resource, annual leave.

4.1.3. Ordering

E.g. books, desks, catering, stationery, travel.

4.1.4. Request for Change

---

[1] From the author's http://www.itskeptic.org/list-request-classes-help-out-itil

As defined by change management, typically means change to a CI. Some organisations allow users to open RFCs directly; others have some form of prior request entity.

4.1.5. Work
Tasks that falls outside change management. E.g. run a report, move a PC, install a projector.

4.2. Support
The user wants our assistance.

4.2.1. Incident
A user perceives an unplanned interruption to an IT service or reduction in the quality of an IT service.

4.2.2. Fault
Failure or detected imminent failure of a CI, no service impact (yet). Only users within IT would be expected to report these, or an automated tool. If confirmed, it will spawn a Problem.

4.2.3. Help
E.g. correcting bad data arising from user error; restoring a deleted file; untangling a mess...

4.2.4. Advice
How do I ... ? Should I ... ? Which is the best way to ... ?

4.3. Input
The user is contributing

4.3.1. Proposal
The service desk can be a front-end to the demand component of project portfolio management. Think of it as a Request For Project.

4.3.2. Suggestion
Idea, requirement, request. Something less formal or evolved than a proposal but might lead to one.

4.3.3. Feedback
Praise, reported experience, remarks

4.3.4. Complaint
Poor experience.

Glossary

Adaptive Case Management (**ACM**): case management where the system changes in response to the external environment to make the practice more successful, learning from past cases to improve approach, models, knowledge, templates, checklists or procedures

accreditation: renewable professional recognition by a reputable organisation of the skills, experience and character of a practitioner.

Business Process Modelling (BPM): a formal system (BPM Notation, BPMN) of diagrammatically describing organisational processes.

case: A case is a situation needing to be responded to, which is not covered by a standardised process model.

Case Management: is the science of managing cases, a body of knowledge that exists in different forms in other sectors such as medicine and law.

certification: acknowledgement of a certain skill or knowledge level, usually by passing an examination or assessment.

Change Management: A much-used term: can mean anything from organisational transformation to control of updates to production IT environments.

checklist: A list of things to be done, not necessarily implying any order.

Capability Maturity Model (CMM): now known as CMMI (never mind). A 5-level means of assessing how well a practice is managed (not performed).

cold case: a case that is still open but appears to be unresolvable

Content Management: Organising information, usually in digital files.

Customer Relationship Management (CRM): Can refer to the practice of managing the relationship with client(s), or the tools to do it with.

customer: the stakeholders who pay for the services, as distinct from the users who consume them.

exception: a condition that is unexpected.

gamification: the use of online game ideas and principles to engage and motivate workers

Information Technology (IT): the function that protects and serves the enterprise's use of technology to store and use information.

Information Technology Infrastructure Library (ITIL): the leading best practice body of knowledge on service management for IT.

Lean: Lean is an attitude, a holistic approach, especially to developing strategy but also to planning and designing tactical systems. Lean is about accomplishing more with less: less physical resources (which overlaps the current trend towards everything "green"), less cost, less time, less effort. It focuses on stripping systems and processes down to only what is required to deliver what the customer wants and to maximise the delivered value. Put another way, Lean eliminates waste. Waste appears in the following forms: Overprocessing, Transportation, Motion, Inventory, Waiting, Defects, and Overproduction. Some speak of the "8th Waste", the waste of human potential due to poor morale, lack of training, or inefficient allocation.

longitudinal: keeps a single picture of the subject over that subject's lifecycle, managed as one case.

RACI: a chart mapping roles to activities, where the mapping is either Responsible, Accountable, Consulted or Informed. Also known as RASCI, with the additional role of Supporting.

Resolve: the step of the generic response process which seeks to find a resolution. This step is (optionally) involves case management.

Response: any situation or "ticket" which requires a human response, such as Request, Incident, Problem, Change, Event.... I have tried to limit responses in time and scale, e.g. a project to build a new system is not treated as a response – it is something that may be initiated/triggered by a response.

Root Cause Analysis (RCA): Determining the causes of something that happened.

Service Desk: a business function - i.e. a team with their own roles, procedures, tools and metrics – that provides response to users.

Service Level Agreement (SLA): An agreement between two business entities for one to provide a service to the other, and the expectations of the utility and warranty of that service. It may be contractual or informal, explicit or implicit.

Service Level Target (SLT): A metric that is measured as a target to quantify the expected service level in an SLA.

Service Management: The body of knowledge that describes how reality works in a service economy. SM is not a theory among many; it is the description of reality.

Six Sigma: A method of improving quality by removing the causes of defects (errors) and minimising statistical variance. The name comes from sigma, the symbol for standard deviation. Skilling up a number of experts in its methods is an important part of introducing Six Sigma, known as Six Sigma "black belts".

SM-Case: this author's term for the particular flavour of case management as applied to service management. SM-Case is the "case" half of Standard+Case.

supplier: A business entity that provides a service to a customer.

Taylor, Taylorism: a theory of "scientific management" founded by Frederick Taylor that analysed and synthesised workflows to improve efficiency, especially labour productivity.

template: An artefact, usually a document that provides a shape to an expected action or output.

ticket: an electronic work record of a situation which requires a human response.

Total Quality Management (TQM). A theory of quality improvement much used in manufacturing industries. TQM is based on the concept that everybody at all points in the value chain needs to be involved in improving the quality of the product or service.

user: An IT term for the stakeholder that consumes a service. Most other sectors say "client".

Bibliography

Guide to the Universal Service Management Body of Knowledge (USMBOK), I Clayton, Service Management 101; 2012.03a edition (2008), ISBN-13: 978-0981469102

Human Interactions: The Heart and Soul of Business Process Management, K Harrison-Broninski, Meghan Kiffer Pr (2005), 978-0929652443

How Knowledge Workers Get Things Done, L Fischer ed., Future Strategies Inc. 2012, 978-0-98497644-7

How to Measure Anything, D W Hubbard, Wiley 2007, 978-0-47011012-6

ITIL *Service Operation*, Cabinet Office, TSO 2011, 978-0-11331307-5

ITIL *Service Transition*, Cabinet Office, TSO 2011, 978-0-11331306-8

Kanban and Scrum, H Kniberg, M Skarin, C4media 2010, 978-0557-13832-6

Management Challenges for the 21st Century, P. Drucker, Butterworth-Heinemann 2007 2nd Ed, 978-075068509-2

Mastering the Unpredictable, K D Swenson, Meghan-Kiffer Press 2010, 978-092965212-2

The Checklist Manifesto, A Gawande, metropolitan 209, 978-0-80509174-8

The Practice of Management, P Drucker, Harper-Collins 1954, 0-06-011095-3

Thinking for a Living, T. Davenport, Harvard Business School Press 2005, 978-159139423-5

Index

About the author

Rob England is an IT commentator and consultant. He consults in New Zealand on IT governance, strategy and processes. Internationally, he is best known for his blog The IT Skeptic and half a dozen books on IT, and he speaks widely at conferences and online. Rob was the NZ IT Service Management Champion for 2010 and his blog was voted the best "IT consultant and analyst" blog in the UK's Computer Weekly IT Blog Awards for 2010. He is an acknowledged contributor to ITIL (2011 *Service Strategy* book).

Rob's other books (www.twohills.co.nz/books) include:

Basic Service Management

A 50 page description of how to plan and provide services, or put another way: how to manage your organisation. Service Management is the potent idea that could change the way you run your organisation. This useful little book is a guide to operating any enterprise, from the point of view of the services it delivers. After all, delivery is what success is about. Also available in Spanish.

Owning ITIL®

Essential reading for all decision makers (IT-literate or not) who are presented with an ITIL® proposal or who are asked to oversee an ITIL project, or who find something called "ITIL" or "Service Management" in their budget. It tells you what the ITIL industry won't. For everyone else involved in ITIL projects, this book is just as essential to help you through the ITIL minefield.

Working in IT

Ideas and inspiration to think about your own career and the careers of those who work for you, and to make a difference in both.

Introduction to Real ITSM

It is not often that ITSM books are funny, but - according to readers - this one is funny. Real ITSM is a tongue-in-cheek satirical look at what the real-life processes of IT Service Management might be, as compared to the "official" defined processes.

Made in the USA
San Bernardino, CA
12 January 2016